THE POCKET GUIDE TO
BEER

Michael Jackson is recognized as the world's leading authority on beer styles. For his previous book *The World Guide to Beer*, the definitive work on that topic, he was honoured in the Literary Awards of the German Academy of Gastronomy in 1978. He has contributed to the Food and Wine pages of the London *Evening Standard*, and his humorous essays have appeared in leading newpapers in Britain and the U.S. He publishes his own newsletter in the U.S., *Michael Jackson's Private Guide to Imported Beers*, and has conducted many tastings and lectures.

THE POCKET GUIDE TO
BEER

MICHAEL JACKSON

Frederick Muller Limited
London

To Pat, for seeing me through the year

First published in Great Britain in 1982 by Frederick Muller
Limited, Dataday House, London, SW19 7JU

ISBN: 0-584-95013-6 (hardcover)
      0-584-95015-2 (softcover)

The Pocket Guide to Beer
was produced and prepared by
Quarto Marketing Ltd.
212 Fifth Avenue, New York, New York 10010

Editor: John Smallwood
Production Editor: Gene Santoro
Designer: Christine Goulet
Design Assistant: Elizabeth Fox
Illustrations by Anne Winters
Cover Design: Ken Diamond

Printed and bound in the United States of America by
Maple-Vail Group

CONTENTS

INTRODUCTION	1
TYPES OF BEERS	4
PROPERTIES OF A GOOD BEER	12
CZECHOSLOVAKIA	24
GERMANY	28
SCANDINAVIA	48
BELGIUM	53
THE NETHERLANDS	66
BRITAIN AND IRELAND	71
FRANCE	91
OTHER EUROPEAN COUNTRIES	95
CANADA	102
THE UNITED STATES	106
LATIN AMERICA	125
AUSTRALASIA	127
ASIA AND AFRICA	131
INDEX OF BREWERIES AND BRANDS	135

ACKNOWLEDGEMENTS

Some of the most genuinely modest men I have ever met are great brewers. I am in awe of them, as I would be of a great chef, and I am forever grateful for the interest that many of them have taken in my researches. Others have been less helpful. Some brewing companies are content to brandish the mashing fork and lyricize about their history, or to take refuge in their "modern and well-equipped plant", and others are irrationally secretive. Several of the brewers whose products I most admire have been recalcitrant to the point of discourtesy. I have made every effort nonetheless to do justice to their beers, and not to favour those made by more friendly brewers. I thank everyone who has helped, in breweries, trade associations, and national tourist organizations. I also thank my editors Charlie Papazian (*Zymurgy*, magazine of the American Homebrewers' Association, Boulder, CO) and Brian Glover (*What's Brewing*, newspaper of the Campaign for Real Ale, St Albans, Herts), and my fellow authors Roger Protz and Frank Baillie, all of whom have helped spread the word. Last, but perhaps most of all, my thanks to the following enthusiasts, who went to special lengths to help make this book a reality:

The United States
Alan Dikty and Larry Popelka
Karl von Knoblauch

Britain
Hugh Llewelyn
John Telfer
John Westlake

The Netherlands
Nico van Dijk

Belgium
Paul Sher

Germany
Brigitte Krauter

INTRODUCTION

This book has been designed as a reference for the drinker who is confronted by a startling growth in the number of beers available and in some (though not all) markets, a bewilderment of choice. This phenomenon is evident in the U.S., Britain, The Netherlands, Belgium, France and several other countries. Each of these lands imports beers from at least some of the others, and within all of them regional beers are increasingly becoming available farther from home.

The Pocket Guide to Beer has sought to consider all brews which are to any great extent available internationally, but it has also given attention to local products which are of special interest for their quality, style or heritage. For ease of reference, beers are grouped within their nations of origin (though there is also a comprehensive index). The sections dealing with the larger brewing nations are then divided into regions to showcase differences in stylistic emphasis, in much the way that a guide to wines would distinguish in France between those of Bordeaux and Burgundy.

THE SELECTION OF BEERS

Almost every nation in the world, except a handful with rigid religious constraints, produces at least one beer, but there are perhaps 20 countries or regions which have significant brewing traditions, and half a dozen of those are of particular interest. Those are the areas which are dealt with at special length. Among them, the largest producing nation in volume is the U.S., but it has only about 40 independent brewing companies. In deference to the volume of beer produced in the U.S., and taking into account the small number of brewing companies, all of them have been given some consideration though subsidiaries with similar product ranges are usually ignored. This round figure of 40 brewing companies has then been applied on a selective basis to countries like Britain, Belgium, and Germany, each of which has far more. Germany, with 1,364 breweries, would merit a dense study indeed if it were to be covered comprehensively. To avoid repetition, companies whose products are brewed in several different nations, either by branch plants or under license, are all considered under their native country.

STRENGTH RATINGS

Brewers are not generally required to indicate the strengths of their beers on their labels, though it would be a good idea if they were. In the U.S., where brewers are subject to state laws, a nationally marketed beer will differ in strength depending upon the part of the country in which it is sold. These laws also affect the availability of imports, and the ways in which they are labelled. In some European countries, beers are labelled with their original gravities, or in categories (eg I, II, III, Superior), relating to broad bands of alcoholic strength. Where possible I have established the strengths of beers discussed, and in the British market especially, where a naturally conditioned beer may vary slightly in potency from one day to another, I have sought to quote original gravities. Typical strengths are also set out at the beginning of each major chapter as a rule of thumb, where no specific information has been unearthed.

BEER STRENGTHS IN THE U.S.

The alcohol contents cited here are measured according to weight, as is customary in the U.S. This system furthers the notion that these beers are especially weak. Some other countries, notably Canada, express alcohol content by volume, which produces higher figures. Typical U.S. beers might provide the following figures under systems used in other parts of the world. Figures vary from brewery to brewery and state to state. These figures are averaged out over a large number of different breweries.

	By weight	By volume	British gravity	European gravity
Lite beer	3.2%	4.0%	1030	7.5°
Regular beer	3.5%	4.37%	1044	11.25°
Premium beer	3.9%	4.87%	1050	12.5°
Super-premium	4.2%	5.25%	1052	13.3°
Specialties	4.5–6.5%	5.6–8.1%	1056–1068	13–17°

QUALITY RATINGS

Each entry discusses the most interesting beers produced by that particular brewer. Only if the brewer has a relatively small range will his entire product line be discussed. Light beers, even if they are mentioned, are not generally accorded a rating, but products of any substance are awarded a number of stars, according to the following system:

***** = world classic
**** = highly distinctive
*** = worthy of attention
** = a well-made beer
* = average

It is argued that gastronomic preferences are subjective, but no one can deny that a Premier Cru Bordeaux is likely to have more complexity and distinction than a jug wine (or, in the British phrase, a "plonk"). The same is true among beers. A beer rated ***** is a world classic either because it has outstanding complexity and distinction or because it is the definitive example of its style, and no matter whether everyone is capable of appreciating it; some people probably don't like first-growth Bordeaux, either. A beer rated **** is highly distinctive among its compatriot products, though it might not be if it were to appear in another market. The same caveat is to be taken into account in respect of lesser ratings, too, though a tenuous effort has been made to reflect the differences in standards from one country to another. The whole scale of ratings in the German section tends to be high because all beers in that country are of what must be recognized internationally as a particularly good quality. Specialty products in Belgium, and almost all cask-conditioned ales in Britain are of such great individuality that few get less than ***.

These ratings are not intended so much to praise or bury the beer as to guide the reader, and help indicate what might be expected of the product.

TYPES OF BEERS

Just as wines may be categorized as red, rosé, or white, dry or sweet, sparkling or still, by geographical origin, or by the name of the producer, so beers also divide into distinct styles.

THE "REDS" AND THE "WHITES"

The most important distinction in style is between what might loosely be regarded as the "red wines" and the "white wines" of the beer world. This central division is based not on colour but on the way in which the beers are made.

The stylistic division between the "reds" and "whites" arose because beers produced by the original method called top fermentation, were, and still are, less stable. The yeast rises to the top during fermentation: before the invention of refrigeration, brews were very unstable in warm weather. The solution was to cease brewing in summer, and to store reserve stocks of beer somewhere cold. In Bavaria, the Alpine caves provided an excellent storage place. The brewers also noticed that, after some months in these conditions, the beer gained a permanent stability because the yeast had sunk to the bottom of the brew. From at least the 15th century, the Bavarian brewers employed this technique empirically, and with their greater understanding of yeast and the development of refrigeration, during the last century they were able to do so methodically. Such bottom fermentation was perfected by their neighbours in Vienna and Pilsen.

The "red wines" are produced by top fermentation, and include all genuine ales; porters and stouts; all Belgian specialty beers; the local styles of German cities like Cologne, Düsseldorf, and Münster; and all wheat beers. There is no generic term for these beers. They usually have a big, assertive palate, irrespective of whether they are thin-bodied or full, low in alcohol or strong. Most are copper or dark brown in colour, but there are notable exceptions. The way in which these beers are best served is influenced by the techniques used in their production. They are fermented, and often matured, at relatively high temperatures, and in consequence some of them better express their palate if they are not chilled. It is for this reason, and not through eccentricity or laziness, that these types of beer are often served at a natural cellar temperature.

The "white wines" of the beer world are produced by bottom fermentation. This category embraces the local styles of Pilsen, Vienna, Munich (including bock beers), and Dortmund. These can all be generically defined as lagers. The term derives from the German word **lager**, meaning store. A good lager beer is stored for between one and three months while it matures. This period of lagering is carried out at about 0°–2° C (32°–36° F) and the beers are usually served chilled. Lager beers are, with certain exceptions, less assertive, typically clean-tasting and quenching. Although there are dark brown and copper-coloured lagers, the golden pilsener style is the most familiar internationally.

The popularity of the original pilsener was well deserved, but its renown is ill served by the many brewers in different parts of the world who have used indifferent imitations to try to create a single international beer style at the expense of more characterful regional specialties. It is as though the whole world were to drink Rhine wines and forget about the very existence of Burgundy and Bordeaux. The "whites" of the beer world are more stable and consistent, but top-fermenting yeasts endow the "reds" with greater personality.

THE LANGUAGE OF THE LABEL

BOTTOM-FERMENTING BEERS

LAGER Any bottom-fermenting beer.

PILSENER (various spellings). Golden-coloured lager. Hop emphasis in the palate. A salty digestif quality similar to that found in Perrier water is pronounced in the original Czech Pilsner Urquell. This beer also has a slightly tannic house character, probably deriving from its having been aged in wood. These two characteristics are not necessarily to be found in otherwise similar Czech beers, like that of Budweis. German pilsener-type beers are sometimes even more hoppy than the original, and thus very dry. Pilsener-type beers from elsewhere can be disappointingly bland. The indication "12°" on the Urquell Pilsner label refers to density (see p. 2) and not alcohol content (around 4% w; 5% v).

MÜNCHNER Dark brown, malt-accented lager of the type originated in Munich. Brewed in many parts of the world, it is often a rather neglected specialty. What in the U.S. is known simply, and with unsatisfactory vagueness, as a "dark beer" often, but not always, turns out to be a Münchner. In its home city, this style is also identified as a "dark" (dunkel) beer, but mainly to distinguish it from an otherwise similar Munich-type malty, pale beer known as a helles. Like big beer-drinkers in several other parts of the world, the people of Munich, and Bavaria in general, temper the high quantity with relatively low strength. On their home ground, Münchner beers are inclined to be around 3.5 percent alcohol by weight, 4.3 percent by volume.

DORTMUNDER A golden-coloured balancing act between the maltiness of Munich beer and the hoppiness of Pilsen beer, and slightly stronger than either. However, the traditional local style of Dortmund has been slipping in strength and is currently around 4.2 percent alcohol by weight, 5.2 percent by volume. Because this local Dortmunder style was once shipped widely in Germany, it is known as Export within its home city. The city's brewers also aggressively market beers of other styles, especially pilsener, the type they are inclined to export today.

VIENNA A copper-coloured lager, notably full-bodied and with malt emphasis. Originally the local style of the city but now more widely represented by the *Märzen* (March) or *Oktoberfest* brews of Munich. Alcohol content is around 4.5 percent by weight, 5.6 percent by volume.

BOCK Originally this was a designation for the strongest of German beers, brewed in the city of Einbeck, in Lower Saxony. The last syllable of Einbeck is supposed to have been corrupted to "bock" by the people of Munich, who took up the style. Since bock also means billy-goat, this type of beer has become vaguely associated with the astrological sign of Capricorn. This connection is consolidated by those brewers who produce bock beers in December, though there is also a strong seasonal tradition in Germany that insists that March, April, and especially May are the months for this type of drink. Several justifications are advanced for festive samplings of bock beer at certain times of the year, but it seems most likely that the tradition originates as in the case of Märzen beer, from the days when it was impossible to brew in warm weather: the last stored beer of summer might have been drained as an autumn bock, and the final new brew of winter in May. A German bock has an alcohol content of not less than 5.0 percent by weight and 6.25 percent by volume, and often more. Some brewers produce both pale and dark bocks.

By some perverse inversion, the term bock is sometimes used in Belgium and France to indicate a beer of low strength. It seems that these beers, being easily consumed in large quantities, were in the past often served in big, German-style glasses, from which the designation was derived.

DOPPELBOCK This "double" bock is a separate classification. A German doppelbock has not less than 6.0 percent alcohol by weight and 7.5 percent by volume. The strongest type, with 13.2 percent alcohol by volume, is eisbock. *Eis* means ice. During preparation, the beer is frozen. Because water freezes before alcohol does, the removal of ice concentrates the strength of the beer, although the end product is rather disagreeably rich. The first doppelbock was created in Munich by the monastic brewery of St. Francis of Paula, and was named Salvator, after the Saviour. The monastery brewery was the forerunner of today's Paulaner-Thomas-Bräu, which still produces Salvator. Inspired by this beer, all other brewers of doppelbocks give them names ending in *–ator*. In Munich alone, Löwenbräu has its Triumphator, Spatenbrau its Optimator, the Hofbrauhaus its Delicator, Augustiner its Maximator, and Hacker-Pschorr its Animator.

DIET PILS This is low-carbohydrate beer for diabetics. The "diet" has nothing to do with slimming, though many drinkers like to believe that it does. People who enjoy very dry beers like it on the merits of its palate, irrespective of health considerations.

The dryness of diet pils results from a lack of sugars in the end product. Originally, malt sugars are present in the same quantity as in a normal beer, but become converted to alcohol by a thorough attenuation, perhaps brought about by an unusually long period of primary fermentation or a very heavy krausening, though processes vary. Diet beers thus have, in relation to the original amount of malt from which they are brewed, an unusually high alcohol content, typically around 4.75 percent by weight and 6.0 by volume. This type of beer was popularized in Germany, and is widely marketed in Britain. In the U.S., there are stricter laws against any labeling that might be construed as indicating health benefits.

LIGHT BEERS Low-calorie beers in the U.S. and, to a lesser extent, Britain, use this designation. These are simply very weak beers. "Extra lights" have been marketed in the U.S. with an alcohol content as low as 2.3 by weight, 2.8 by volume, but the most popular brands have about 3.2 by weight, 4.0 by volume. At these low strengths, it is difficult to brew a lager with any taste. One solution is to hop more heavily than usual. Another is to brew to a high strength, then dilute. This technique, known as high-gravity brewing, is also used by some companies to maximize their production of conventional beers. Because it alters the natural balance that takes place in brewing, it also affects taste; whether to the good is an open question.

TOP-FERMENTING BEERS

ALE The British type of beer, of which the defining characteristic is production by top-fermentation. Ales typically
have a very pronounced palate derived from the use of
top-fermenting yeasts. Ale remains the most popular style
of beer in Britain, and in muted form sometimes exists in
one or two other parts of the world as a result of British
influence. Ales can be made to any strength, and the
designation has nothing to do with alcohol content,
although in the U.S. it is sometimes used in this way at
the behest of state liquor authorities.

CREAM ALE A U.S. term, despite spurious suggestions of Irish
origin. The best-known label is, in fact, a blend of a small
proportion of true ale with a larger amount of lager beer.

PORTER This London beer style was preeminent throughout
Britain from the mid-17th century to the mid-18th century but was then ousted by pale ales of the style
popularized by brewers in the Midlands town of Burton.
Porter remained popular in Ireland, especially the north,
well into the 20th century, but production ceased completely in 1973. The style was revived in 1978 by a couple
of English brewers. Still, porter remains harder to find in
its native country than it is, to varying degrees of
authenticity, in some other parts of the world, including
the U.S.. Porter derives its very dark brown colour and
characteristic bitterness from the use of roasted, unmalted barley. Its bitterness is also heightened by a very
high hopping rate, producing some acidity in the palate.
Traditionally, it is top-fermented and well-attenuated,
producing a very firm but thin palate.The original porters
were regarded as beers of medium strength.

STOUT A fuller-bodied, richer, and traditionally stronger
brother brew to porter, and again made with the use of
roasted, unmalted barley. Of the two types, stout has
survived much better. It manifests itself in two main
styles: the dry, Irish version typified by Guinness, and the
sweet, English rendition exemplified by Mackeson.The
dry style is also made by Murphy's and Beamish, both in
Ireland, and by one or two brewers elsewhere in the
world. Mixed half and half with Champagne, it is the basis
of a black velvet, one of the most refreshing and luxurious
drinks known to man or woman. The sweet style, sometimes described colloquially as milk stout, is held to be
especially nutritious (versions fortified with oatmeal or
oyster essence have also been produced). Sweet stouts
are made by a good many British brewers. A third and
more specialized designation of stout is the Imperial type
originally brewed for export, by way of the Baltic Sea, to
the Russian Empire of the Tsars. These stouts were
brewed to very high gravities and allowed to ferment on
the high seas, arriving strong enough to warm the coldest

Russian winter. There is some doubt about the future of the classic version, brewed in Britain today by Courage, but Imperial-style stouts are also produced in Denmark and Finland.

ALT The German counterpart to ale. Even the name is similar, although alt simply means old, a reminder that this beer is made by top-fermentation, the "old" method predating the lager revolution of the mid-18th century. Germany did most to popularize lager beer, although geographically that current came from southeast Germany, and was resolutely ignored by several brewing cities in faraway northwest Germany. The brewers of the northwest still brew in their "old" way, and their beers have not only survived as the dominant home-town styles but are also increasing in popularity.

These beers have a modest alcohol content of 3.5–4.0 percent by weight, 4.3-5.0 by volume, a rounded, hoppy palate, and is less yeasty than its English cousins. Altbiers typically have a rich copper colour, but a single pale golden version is produced in the town of Münster by the Pinkus Müller home-brew house.

KÖLSCH The characteristic beer of Cologne, after which it is named. Ten or a dozen breweries in the Cologne-Bonn metropolitan area specialize in this distinctive, top-fermenting style, and are so proud of it that they have gone to the law to prevent anyone else using the designation Kölsch.

The beer is unusually pale in colour, with a complex hop character, a slightly lactic palate, and a soft, low carbonation. Kölsch has an alcohol content of about 3.7 percent by weight, 4.6 by volume.

SAISONS A regional specialty in the French-speaking part of Belgium, and in seasonal terms the top-fermenting counterpart to the springtime beers of Germany. Saisons are brewed from a high original gravity, and their sharpness is rounded by a long period of warm conditioning, followed by a *dosage* of yeast in the bottle. Saison is often presented in a wine-shaped, corked liter bottle, out of which it is liable to surge like Champagne. They have a big, rocky head, a copper colour, and a fresh, fruity palate. The most widely available example, Saison Régal, has an alcohol content of just over 4.5 percent by weight, 5.6 percent by volume, but many of the lesser-known labels are notably stronger.

TRAPPIST ABBEY BEERS Although there are monastery breweries in other countries, five Trappist abbeys in Belgium and a sixth across the Dutch border have established their own stylistic tradition of very strong fruity top-fermenting beers that are conditioned in the bottle. Although these six abbeys produce about a dozen beers, each different and varying in strength from about 4.6–9.6

percent by weight, 5.7–12.0 by volume, the brews have enough in common for the designation Trappist to have some meaning.

BIÈRE DE GARDE This regional style of northern France seems to be enjoying a welcome revival after having been on the brink of disappearance. Always presented in a wine-shaped, corked bottle, these "laying-down" beers are made with a blend of pale Pilsen and dark Munich malts in a single-stage mash, producing a rich amber brew. They were traditionally top-fermented, and still aspire to that character although they are more commonly made with bottom yeasts and cold-conditioned. They are rich and malty, but smooth rather than sticky, usually with an alcohol content of 4.4–4.8 percent by weight, 5.5-6.0 by volume. Outside of France, the most commonly found examples are St. Léonard and Lutèce.

BERLINER WEISSE The name means the white beer of Berlin. The beer isn't really that colour, but it is very pale, sometimes cloudy, with a very white head. It has a secondary fermentation induced by the addition of a lactic culture, and creates an immense mousse. This elegant traditional specialty is intended as a quenching summer drink, and is thus lightly hopped and brewed to a low alcohol content of 2.0–3.0 percent by weight, 2.5–3.75 by volume. It is served in large bowl-shaped glasses that might be expected to contain a fruit salad. To the further astonishment of those not familiar with the style, it is laced with a dash of raspberry syrup or green essence of woodruff. Although this style belongs to Berlin, similar weisse beers are produced elsewhere in Germany. "White" wheat beers are also made in Belgium, in the area east of Brussels, where they are a tradition in the town of Louvain and the village of Hoegaarden.

WEIZENBIER This means simply wheat beer, and is the un-fancy term used by the brewers in south Germany for their contribution to the genre. While the weisse beer of the north is made with a mash containing only a quarter wheat, the weizen brewers of the south use at least a third, and often more. Sometimes, they employ twice as much wheat as barley. While the Berlin beer is deliber-ately low in alcohol, those of Bavaria and Baden-Württemberg vary from medium to strong. The northern wheat beer is very light, but those of the south have a big, malty bouquet and some hop bitterness. They are served in tall, narrow, vase-shaped glasses, usually with a slice of lemon, although some drinkers eschew this embellish-ment.

A typical wheat-beer brewer in the south may produce several variations on the theme. These might include the brewery's own, heavier interpretation of a "white" beer, a weissbier, and perhaps three versions of a weizenbier: a conventional example; one that is unfiltered, so that it is mit hefe ("with yeast"—many drinkers in south Germany like the sediment); and a version up to bock strength. A weizenbock has at least 5.0 percent alcohol by weight, 6.25 by volume, and often more.

LAMBIC The strangest of all beer styles. A family of wheat beers into which the brewer pitches no yeast to promote fermentation, but allows the natural microflora in the atmosphere to do the job, in much the way they do for the producers of wine. Hardly surprisingly, these spontaneously fermenting beers have a markedly vinous character.

Beers genuinely made by this method have been successfully produced only in the valley of the River Senne, west of Brussels. Scientific researchers investigating the properties of this valley still have much to learn, but one of the microflora there have been dubbed, with civic pride, *Brettanomyces bruxelliensis*. Another, *Brettanomyces lambicus*, gives its name to the beer. Lambic itself, the parent style, is very vinous and has an alcohol content of about 3.6 percent by weight, 4.5 by volume. A version sweetened with sugar and sometimes diluted is known as faro. If two lambics are blended, they start a new fermentation, producing a fruity beer called gueze, which has a Champagne sparkle and an alcohol content of about 4.4 percent by weight, 5.5 by volume. If the new fermentation is induced instead by the addition of cherries or raspberries, the magnificent beers produced are called kriek and framboise respectively. Because the fruit is added as a fermentable material, alcohol is boosted to about 4.8 percent by weight, 6.0 by volume.

PROPERTIES OF A GOOD BEER

The fine art of wine-making might be described with brutal simplicity as the crushing of grapes and the fermentation of their juices. Put almost as baldly, the basic steps in the production of beer are as follows:

1. The principal raw material, **barley**, is encouraged to sprout, by being steeped in water, and is then heated in a kiln to produce **malt**. This is done in a building called a **maltings**.
2. In the brewhouse, hot water is added to the malt (sometimes with other cereals) to produce a **mash**. The vessel used is known as a **mash tun**.
3. The mash is clarified, the resultant liquid being referred to as wort. A clarifying vessel known as a lauter tun may be used.
4. The wort is transferred to a vessel known as a kettle or copper, where it is boiled. This is the actual brewing process.
5. During brewing, hops are added, primarily as a bittering agent, though they also help clarify and preserve the brew.
6. The hops are removed and the wort cooled and transferred out of the brewhouse to the fermentation vessels.
7. Yeast is added (this is known as pitching) to produce primary fermentation.
8. When this has ceased, the fermented wort is moved again to be matured or aged, often with a secondary fermentation, in lagering tanks or casks.
9. The beer is filtered unless it is to be permitted to condition further in the bottle or cask.
10. If it is to be pasteurized, this process takes place at the bottling, canning, or kegging stage.

At every one of these stages, brewers have their own additional procedures or variations of ingredients, treatments, time, and temperatures. Fundamental variations make for different styles of beer; personal touches of craftsmanship add finesse to all types of beer.

Strength This characteristic is often misleadingly taken as the measure of a beer. Yet the drinker who samples a weisse beer should not complain that the beer is so weak he could drink it all afternoon—that is the idea. Strength is not virtue in beer any more than in life. Strong beers are essential to those who wish to get drunk in haste, but they do have more particular purposes. Like a single-malt Scotch, a strong beer warms the heart after a winter's walk, or calms the mind at nightfall. A beer meant to soothe is made in a different manner from one intended to refresh. Each must be judged according to its style.

TYPICAL BEER STRENGTHS

Alcohol*	U.S.	Britain	Germany
	Extra lights		
3.0 (2.4)			
	Lights	*Milds*	*Berliner weisse*
3.5 (2.8)		*Sweet stouts*	
		Bitters	
4.0 (3.2)			
		Dry stouts	*Müncheners*
4.5 (3.6)			
	Regular beers	*Best bitters*	*Pilseners*
5.0 (4.0)	*US ales*	*Pale ales*	*Dortmunders*
	Malt liquors		*Weizenbiers*
5.5 (4.4)			
		Old ales	*Oktoberfests*
6.0 (4.8)			
		Barley wines	*Bocks*
6.5 (5.2)			
7.0 (5.6)			
7.5 (6.0)			
			Doppelbocks
8.0 (6.4)			
	Strongest malt liquors		
8.5 (6.8)			
9.0 (7.3)			
9.5 (7.6)			
10.0 (8.0)			
10.5 (8.4)			
		Strong barley wine	
11.0 (8.8)			
11.5 (9.2)			
12.0 (9.6)			
12.5 (10.0)			
		Thomas Hardy's ale	
13.0 (10.4)			
			Kulminator

*by vol (by weight) © Michael Jackson

Below ....
Above

The nose Aroma is far more important in a beer than is commonly realised. Good brewers take a good deal of trouble over the nose, or bouquet, of their beer. The nose is influenced by three principal factors, the most obvious being the hop. The manner in which a beer is hopped usually takes into account the fact that its aroma can greatly enhance the perception of taste. The main hopping, which is intended to impart the required degree of dryness and bitterness, takes place in the brew-kettle or copper, just before the boil (the vessel may be called a copper even if it is made from stainless steel). However, many brewers have one or more subsequent hopping stages. Hops may be added right at the end of the boil, to add aroma. These are known as finishing hops. There may be a further very light hopping during maturation so that the nose is intensified. Because this takes place after the full fury of brewing, in the time of quiet maturation, it is known as **dry-hopping**. The handful of hops added at this stage is not boiled to bitterness but gently gives of itself, especially in aroma.

Hop character At each of these stages, a different variety of hop, or a different blend of hops, may be added. In the brewing of Budweiser, eight varieties are used in three different blends. The variety or blend used for finishing or dry-hopping will be the most evident in the bouquet. Among the varieties often used for this purpose, the Saaz hops of Czechoslovakia are the most delicate and complex; the Hallertaus of Bavaria have a superbly firm, earthy, almost spicy character; Brewer's Gold, from Britain, is very big, heavy, and perhaps cloying; the Cascades of the U.S. are geranial, with an oily sweet, minty character.

Any brewer who pays attention to finishing or dry-hopping clearly cares about the beer, so a good hop character in the bouquet is an early indication of a good beer.

Malt aroma The second great component of the bouquet is the malt. If the beer is brewed with a conventional pale malt, and if this has not been diluted into impotence by lesser grains, the aroma will be quite evident. The aroma of malt is what passers-by smell near a brewery, especially on a day when rain is expected and the atmosphere is moist. If darker malts are used, their aroma will speak more of the roasting kiln, like that of espresso coffee or even chocolate.

Fruitiness The third component is a fruity aroma deriving from esters, compounds produced by the yeast during fermentation and maturation. A touch of estery fruitiness is an essential quality in beer, and in some brands and types it is part of the product's character. A hint of sweet corn or parsnip is quite properly found in lagers, as is the very slightest suggestion of apple or

pear. However, if either of these esters becomes assertive, then something has gone seriously wrong, and the
beer should not have been released. The same is true of
an excessive butterscotch aroma, though in a restrained
presence it is an essential quality of ales. Some of the
finest ales have a citric, peachy quality or even a hint of
mulberry or strawberry. In very strong beers, this fruitiness may merge with the slight alcohol nose, becoming
reminiscent of some French *eaux-de-vie*.

A cabbage aroma, on the other hand, suggests a
serious defect. The beer has been around too long,
perhaps on a supermarket shelf, and has been damaged
by light. Any kind of light damages beer—hence the use
of green or brown glass—but the type of illumination
used in supermarkets plays havoc with one of the
molecules that cause hop bitterness and corrupts it
into cabbagey "skunkiness".

An equally unpleasant aroma and taste of damp
paper or cardboard also means that the beer has been
left around for too long. In this instance, the culprit is
oxygen, either present at the time of bottling or allowed
to seep in through a faulty seal. Oxidation damages the
taste of beer by attacking acids derived from the grain
from which it was made. In order to combat this, some
brewers use ascorbic acid as an additive. They would
do better to seal their bottles with greater care and
make sure their beer is not exported over long distances
unless they are sure of a very quick sale.

The head A dense, uneven "rocky" head is a good sign
that a beer has gained its life through natural fermentation, and not by being injected with carbon dioxide.
Another good sign involves what is known as the bead—
the bubbles. If, as the beer is poured, there is an
undignified rush of large bubbles, which quickly sub-
sides, carbonation is artificial. If the bead is smaller,
forming spires that continue to build throughout the
time it takes to drink the beer, it has probably been
brewed with care and attention. It is a further good sign
if the foam sticks to the side of the glass, leaving behind
"Brussels lace". Brewers can use a seaweed extract as
an additive to help retain the foam, but this is not very
effective if the head isn't there in the first place.

How large a head should there be? The Germans like
a "beautiful blooming" head. The Dutch hold two
fingers together horizontally, alongside the rim of the
glass, to ensure that the head has the proper depth. The
British are said to like flat beer, but this isn't true. They
like their pint glass to be completely filled with beer and
not foam, but do expect a head to form above the level
of the rim.

15

Natural carbonation The secondary fermentation, which takes place during the maturation stage, produces natural carbonation, but it is also brought along by a number of traditional techniques. In the production of lager beers, the classical method, which originated in Bavaria, is krausening. This is a technique in which the secondary fermentation is stimulated by the addition of "young" beer. Other means of achieving this, more commonly employed by ale-brewers, are a priming with sugar at this stage, or a second yeasting like the *dosage* used in the production of Champagne. While in most instances the second fermentation is intended to give spritz and finesse to the beer, it plays a much more central role in the development of the character of some regional special ties in Belgium. These beers, in which the second, or on occasion the third, fermentation takes place in the bottle, are thus described by their brewers with some justification as having been made by the méthode champenoise. If none of these methods is used, the beer may simply be permitted to enjoy its natural secondary fermentation in the cask, the carbonation retained by bunging or sealing, the cask. This method is widely used only in Britain.

Pouring If it has a good natural carbonation, a beer needs only to be poured gently and slowly down the side of a tilted glass to produce a head; that is a good test of a beer. Few breweries suggest this technique, however, although the Swiss company Hürlimann does. It is disingenuous of breweries to maintain, as some do, that beer should be poured straight into the center of the glass. Served that sort of violence, any beer will produce an instant head, but not a very honest one.

The body Fullness of body does not indicate strength, and often suggests the opposite. Everyday Scottish beers, for example, are fuller in body than their English counterparts, but slightly lower in alcohol content. If two brews start out with the same proportion of fermentable raw materials (barley and other grains), and one emerges with a fuller body than the other, then it will also be lower in alcohol. The one with the thinner body will have attenuated itself by a greater degree of fermentation, thus converting more of its natural sugars into alcohol.

The proportion of fermentable materials used obviously affects the cost of production of a beer, and is often the basis for taxation.That is why in some countries beer is rated by its original density rather than by its final alcohol content, which is determined by the degree of attenuation.There are a great many systems and scales by which this is measured, but the most common are the British system of original gravity and the continental European system devised by a Czech scientist with the potent name of Balling. The scale of degrees **Balling**, which is also widely used in the U.S., was subsequently refined to provide very similar figures expressed in **degrees Plato**. Beers in the U.S. are also rated according to the alcohol content as a percent of weight and of volume.

The palate Some brewers proudly proclaim that one or more of their products is an all-malt beer. In Germany and a number of other countries, there is no other kind of beer (except the wheat specialties). Under the terms of historic decree and law, malted barley is the only fermentable material that may be used in brewing in these countries. Elsewhere, barley is also the basic grain, but it may be augmented to the proportion of anything from 15 percent to 40 percent by other fermentable materials that are generically known as **adjuncts**. Breweries do not normally boast about their adjuncts, though Anheuser-Busch makes a point of its use of rice in Budweiser, which the company believes contributes to the crispness of its product. Rice tends to be one of the more expensive adjuncts, while the first attraction of most of these materials was originally their availability and therefore cheapness. In the U.S., corn is the most widely used adjunct. The British, with their Caribbean connections, have over the years used a lot of sugar.

Sweetness Beers that lean heavily on lesser grains and sugars manifest in their palate a lack of confidence, sometimes a dirtiness, a sticky character, and at worst a chickenfeed taste. The true malt palate can best be experienced in the full-bodied beers of Bavaria. The malt that makes beer, like the grape that makes wines, is inherently sweet, but in each case the degree to which this characteristic is allowed to endure is a matter of the preference of the producer of the beverage. At their best, malty beers do not deny the sweetness, but neither are they cloying. Although there are some wonderfully assertive all-malt beers throughout Germany and in several other countries, those in the U.S. tend to restrain their potential in keeping with the U.S. lightness of body. Even then, the all-malt character is evident in their remarkable firmness and cleanness of palate.

The brewers of the "purist" products usually demand that their malt be made from two-row barley. There are, in fact, three principal races of barley, distinguished according to the number of rows of grain in each ear. The best-quality malting barleys are inclined to be of the two-row race. Four-row barley is less suitable for the purposes of brewing, but six-row barley is quite widely used. Despite its less exalted status, six-row barley does have its advocates, who argue that it imparts a characterful "roughness" that seems to suit some beers; an analogy appropriate for wine lovers might be the tannic quality in Barbera wine.

Balance The body and soul of beer is the malt from which it is made. Beer is not made from hops; they are the benediction. In a full-bodied beer, there is a natural tendency for the malt to get the upper hand. Full-bodied beers are "meaty" and satisfying: it is easy to understand how the Bavarians can enjoy one as a mid-morning snack. In the thin-bodied beers, the opposite often happens: the hop comes through more strongly. Of course, it depends how much hop is there in the first place, but if the brewer hasn't been stingy with the hop, its presence will be delightfully evident in a leafy dryness. That is why a hoppy English ale makes such a potent aperitif, and why British drinkers often prefer the thinner-bodied "ordinary" bitter to the bigger "special". Some beers are intended to be hoppy and others to be malty, but in every case a balance must be struck. The brewer's intentions, as indicated by the style of the beer, must be taken into account, but the subtlety and complexity with which the brewer achieves this balance is the greatest of all measures of a beer's success.

Bitterness Inexperienced drinkers with strong opinions often complain that beer is bitter. It is supposed to be. That is why hops are added. The purpose of making beer with hops is that they confer a bitterness. They give the beer its dryness to balance the sweetness of the malt. They also have a preservative effect, but that is of minor importance. Before the hop was universally accepted by brewers as a bittering agent, a wide variety of flowers, berries, spices, and tree barks was used. Home brewers in the Nordic countries still use juniper berries, better known for their similar role in the production of gin. One brewer in Belgium continues to employ coriander, which is also used in gin. Although he doesn't use orange peel, like the gin-distillers, the same brewer does employ Curaçao to similar effect. Similar botanicals, along with flowers like camomile and gentian, are used in the production of vermouths, of patent aperitifs like Campari, and of liqueurs like Chartreuse. In beer, as in these other drinks, bittering agents have the property both of arousing the appetite and aiding the digestion. In France, drinkers have been known to add a splash of their own favourite bitter aperitif, Amer Picon, to a glass of beer (which would seem to be the spoiling of two fine drinks).

A brewer who cares about the beer considers the intensity and nature of the bitterness and palate desired when choosing the variety of hops to be used in the copper. The selection of a hop or blend for the copper is as important as the choice made for finishing. The same hops may be used in each blend, but every brewer has his own ideas. The classic German bitter hop is, arguably, the Spalt, very rugged and "raw". The British favour a wide selection, including the intense Northern Brewer and the delightfully named Fuggles and Goldings, both with big broad character. In the United States, where beers are generally blander, Cluster is widely used.

A good many brewers still use the whole hop—the leafy cone, harvested and dried. Others use pellets compacted from the natural hop. The leafy form is certainly the most aesthetically appealing, and that is not a factor to be dismissed. It is also said to confer a fuller flavour, but that is a matter of great debate among brewers. Pellets are more manageable and, in the case of hops sent halfway across the world, easier to transport. That is even truer of hop extracts, but these are not the same thing at all. Whichever method of hopping is used, the bitterness imparted can be measured on a scale recognized among brewers internationally. The number of units of bitterness can vary from around 12 in one of the blander U.S. lagers to as many as 45 in some ales and stouts.

Texture The sweetness, balance, and bitterness of a beer, and all of its other taste characteristics, are affected not only by the malt and hops used but also by the yeast and the water. Yeast imparts to beer not only fruitiness but also liveliness and its own elusive blend of taste and texture. Water can also confer a sense of hardness or softness, either of which may be agreeable or not depending upon the overall character of the beer, and sometimes a pleasant saltiness. In the past, the presence of certain salts in the local water of some towns made them into natural centers for brewing. This is a less important factor today, when the brewer can quite easily adjust the natural salts in the water. Nonetheless, to have a local water that contains the right salts and can be used *au naturel*, or with simple filtration, can only be an advantage.

Maturity There is a depth to a beer that has been properly matured. Beers are sometimes advertised as being slow-brewed, but this is an imprecise claim. It is quite true that care and attention take extra time at every stage of production: the mashing of the grains in hot water (whether of the simple infusion type used in the making of ales or the more elaborate decoction style often employed for lagers), the separating and boiling of the resultant liquid with hops in the copper (this is the actual brewing, and takes only a couple of hours), and the primary fermentation. By the time the first, principal fermentation is finished, the beer will have been in production, depending upon its type, for more than a week, and quite likely more than two weeks. However, the "slow" brewer spends his real time on maturation, or conditioning.

Most of the world's beers are lagers, and it is the defining characteristic of these brews that they have a period in store (that is the meaning of the German word lager) while they mature and come to condition. This process takes place at low temperatures, usually around 0° C (32° F). There is in this time a slower continuation of the fermentation, a sort of cold ripening, in which unwanted harsh flavour characteristics are released from the beer. At the same time, the beer clarifies. The precipitation of the yeasts, known as fining, may be helped during conditioning by the use of wood chips (in the case of lagers) or insinglass, made from the swim-bladder of the sturgeon (in the case of ales). There are various modern substitutes for these methods.

In countries like Britain and the U.S., where lager-brewers are satisfied to "mature" their beer for less than two weeks, anything more than three weeks is a respectable period. In Germany, the birthplace of lager-brewing, a serious beer is matured for between five and twelve weeks. Traditionally, nine months was the gestation period, but in those days beers were heavier. Even today, some very strong specialties in Europe are matured for a year or more. Today, lagering tanks are manufactured from stainless steel, but many wooden ones are still in use. The maturation of beer in wood, even when it is lined with resin, demands that the brewer exercise diligent stewardship. Yet wooden vessels, like open fermenters, sometimes seem to impart to a beer a house character that cannot be replicated in another brewery.

Conditioning Top-fermenting beers are usually conditioned at warmer temperatures, and for far shorter periods than are bottom-fermenting beers, although there are many variations in the treatment, especially in Belgium. The discriminating drinker in Britain insists that the ale be delivered to the pub before its conditioning is completed. It then spends two or three days reaching its peak condition in the cask in the cellar of the pub at a temperature of about 13° C (56°–57° F). Once tapped, such cask-conditioned beer must be consumed within a couple of days. Some bottled ales in Britain have a similar warm conditioning for about ten days before being pasteurized and dispatched from the brewery. The most traditional technique of all is the practice of blending in young beer, priming with sugar, or re-yeasting to start a new fermentation in the bottle. Apart from the méthode champenoise specialties of Belgium, there are a handful of these bottle-conditioned ales in Britain and a growing number in the U.S., where this technique has been reintroduced by the new, tiny, boutique breweries.

The advantage of conditioning a beer, in the cellar of the pub or in the bottle, is that the yeasts are still at work when the product is consumed. The beer is still "alive" and has a palate that cannot be matched by any other method. It has a sharpness and freshness like that found in a living yogurt, especially one consumed in a remote village in the Balkans. The disadvantage is that a living beer is highly unstable, especially if it is subjected to movement and changes of temperature. Bottle-conditioned beers never leave the brewery until they are ready to drink, but they still continue to develop. In a beer of a regular strength, the sugars are consumed relatively quickly by the yeasts. Such a beer may be in prime condition a month after leaving the brewery, and can start to deteriorate after about nine months, producing a sulphury nose.

Vintage beers In a strong, bottle-conditioned beer there are plenty of sugars upon which the yeasts can slowly work for a long period. There are a very few beers that are especially made in this way for laying down, or storing, as wine-lovers store wine. Although their name would suggest it, the French *bières de garde* are not generally brewed in this manner, but in Belgium the Provisie beer made by the Liefmans brewery is truer to its designation. This beer reaches its peak after two years, but continues to mature for another twenty-five years. Another Belgian specialty, the blue-capped version of Chimay Trappist beer, also reaches its peak after two years. To make life easier for the drinker who likes to lay down a few bottles, Chimay indicates the vintage on the cap. In Britain, the Courage brewery always vintage-dated its Imperial Russian Stout on the neck label (sadly, the future of this product is in some doubt). In the U.S., the Anchor Steam Beer brewery dates its Christmas ales, and drinkers are inclined to save good years. Thomas Hardy's Ale, brewed in the novelist's home county of Dorset, England, is presented much like a Cognac or Armagnac, with a serial number for each of the occasional brews. This beer also has a black-label recommending the drinker to lay it down for not less than three years, and preferably four or five. As if this were not a difficult enough request to comply with, the label points out that the beer will improve if kept for 25 years at 12° C (55° F)—a suitable temperature for keeping any top-fermenting vintage beers. If they are to be enjoyed at their best, vintage beers should not be exposed to frequent or sudden changes of temperature, moved frequently, or exposed to bright light.

Keeping qualities Beers made to be laid-down or conditioned in the cask represent a small number of specialties. The majority of beers, including all of those made by the lager process and a good many ales, are brought to maturity at the brewery and filtered, after which they will not improve and are vulnerable to deterioration. There is nothing to be gained and much to be lost in keeping everyday beers. In the case of an unusually strong lager like FeuerFest, the alcohol level is high enough to discourage any unwanted activity in the bottle. This is not true of beers of conventional strength.

Although one such beer, Henry Weinhard's Private Reserve, from the West Coast, is batch-numbered on the label, that is merely meant to stress the "hand-crafted" nature of the product, and definitely not to encourage laying-down. In some instances, a regular lager may turn out to keep well, but much depends on the care with which it was bottled and the handling to which it has been subjected since it left the brewery. In any event, the fresher an everyday beer is, the better it tastes. Some brewmasters, like mothers worried about the welfare of their children, would secretly prefer it if their beers never left the building. Several brewing companies do impose "pull-dates" of around sixty days, after which they recall unsold beer. The deterioration that they fear often manifests itself in the palate, but is usually evident in an unpleasant aroma. As in wine, so in beer—poor condition is readily betrayed and easily recognized by aroma, and tasting is hardly necessary.

Sediment It surprises the uninitiated to learn that sediment can be a sign of quality in a beer, yet it would be taken for granted in a vintage port. A gathering of yeast sediment at the bottom of a beer bottle normally indicates that the product has been bottle-conditioned, and might be expected to have the maturity, finesse, and vigour associated with that process. Whether the sediment should be poured into the glass is a matter for the taste of the drinker. In Germany, the consumer who orders a weizenbier "with yeast" does so with that in view. In Britain, barmaids take great trouble to decant Worthington White Shield without spilling the yeast into the beer. Some drinkers like to take the beer bright, then swallow the yeast separately afterwards. In Australia, Cooper's Sparkling Ale is an ironic misnomer for a beer that seems to retain its yeast in suspension. In a country where most beers are golden bright, the survival of this fine specialty is remarkable, and its hard-core supporters respond by drinking it in as yeasty a manner as possible. In the U.S., the revival of bottle-conditioned beers is so new that there is not yet a tradition.

Most producers of such brews would probably prefer them to be decanted so that their inherent luster may be appreciated. The subtlety and complexity of color in a beer is a sign of quality, and make an important contribution to its aesthetic appeal. Except in the case of bottle-conditioned specialties, beer is meant to be free from sediment or haze. However, even what might seem an offensive haze can, paradoxically, be a sign of a good brew. Beers made with whole hops in generous quantities, or with 100 percent barley malt rather than cheaper grains or syrups, are especially vulnerable to haze. So are beers made without additives. Tannin and an enzyme extracted from the papaya plant are used to protect beer against haze, to which it is especially vulnerable if it is excessively chilled in the supermarket, as it often is in the U.S.. A brew that throws a haze may thus be a hoppy, all-malt beer with no additives. A beer displaying such a chill haze will clarify if left out of the refrigerator for a while, and its palate will usually not have been seriously affected. If it tastes bad or has an unpleasant aroma, the problem is more serious.

Pasteurization Health-obsessed legislators in some parts of the U.S. insist than even beer must be pasteurized, as if it were milk, which in its natural state apparently can endanger health. In the case of beer, this is nonsense. In countries that know about beer, it is left unpasteurized wherever possible. Pasteurization puts an end to all natural life in beer, and in so doing blunts its palate. Pasteurization also flattens hop character. If a beer has been carefully pasteurized, especially by the quick flash method rather than the slower tunnel technique, the damage may be minimal. The worst damage of all is done when beer lingers in the pasteurization tunnel and comes out with a disagreeable toffeyish palate. Brewers who pasteurize argue that the process has no detrimental effect, and that this has been proven in blindfold taste tests. The same brewers, when offered a beer, seek out one that has not been pasteurized. In Germany, draught brews are usually not pasteurized, and neither are a good many bottled beers except for export. In Britain, cask-conditioned draught ales are by definition not pasteurized. Those tap ales that do undergo pasteurization are normally described as keg rather than draught; thus in Britain these two terms have different meanings. Lagers and the majority of bottled beers in Britain are pasteurized. In the U.S., draught beer is not pasteurized, and bottles almost always are, with the exception of the new boutique ales. Because in most parts of the world draught beer is the less likely to have been pasteurized, it is generally preferred by the discriminating beer-drinker. It escapes pasteurization because, traditionally, it is carried only in establishments with a quick turnover. Bottled beers are apt to be pasteurized because they may travel further and be sold in places, such as supermarkets, that carry a large number of brands and have, for each, a slower turnover. Beer is pasteurized to render it stable and not for any health reason. However, even after pasteurization, it is vulnerable to the effects of oxidation and supermarket lighting.

CZECHOSLOVAKIA

The town of Pilsen gave its name to what has become the most widely produced style of beer in the world, the town of Budweis to the biggest-selling brand, and the town of Micholup, re-spelled, to the best-known "super-premium" brew in the United States.

All three towns are in Czechoslovakia, the first two within the province of Bohemia, the last in Slovakia. When they became famous for their beers, this slice of Europe was within the German-speaking part of the Austro-Hungarian Empire. Since then, Budweis and Micholup have re-emerged with their spellings in the Czech language: Cěske Budějovice and Michalovce.

"Pilsener" became a stylistic description after the town's municipal brewery created the world's first pale lager beer in 1842. At the time, all other brews were either copper-coloured or dark brown, and the new brassy-bright beer of Pilsen seemed dramatically different. Its pale colour was celebrated all the more because mass-produced, clear drinking glasses were replacing traditional vessels made of opaque materials such as stoneware and pewter. Thus it was probably its colour that made Pilsener beer famous, although the product also had outstanding qualities of palate and nose, especially in its hop character.

The designation Pilsener was assumed by brewers all over Europe, and later elsewhere in the world, before the town could protect its name, although belated efforts were made to do this. Some small distinction is derived from the fact that the Czechs, in English, usually use the spelling Pilsner, with only one *e*, while the spelling Pilsener is more popular elsewhere.

Czechoslavakia was known for its beer long before the pale Pilsener was born, and in earlier times Bohemia was noted for its wheat brews. The Bohemians seem to have been the first people in Europe to establish brewing as a trade, in about 1088, and were known for the quality of their hops as early as the 9th century. King Wenceslas of Bohemia, who was a Holy Roman Emperor, forbade the export of hop cuttings in an attempt to protect the exclusivity of the local product.

Bohemian hops are internationally famous today, and are the most expensive in the world. They are sometimes described on beer labels as Saaz hops, a reference to the town of Žatec in the heart of the growing area. Czechoslovakian brews also have a reputation in all serious beer-drinking countries, and the original Pilsner product is by far the most popular import in Germany. The Pilsner brewery, and a slightly younger neighbour in the same town, and those of Budweis and Prague are among the better-known names, but the Czech industry has more than 100 breweries, of which about a quarter export their products.

BRANIK, *Prague.* A small brewery noted for a malty, creamy, pale lager of 14° Plato (1056 British; 4.7% w; 5.8% v). This beer is expecially well served at a medieval inn in Prague called the Vulture (*U supa*). Branik is also admired for its 12° dark (Tmavé), which has a particularly fine colour and a tangy palate (around 4.0% w; 5.0% v).This is notably available at the former monastery of St. Thomas, in Prague. The monastery, known in Czech as U Svatého Tomasĕ, is now one of the city's most atmospheric drinking places, with vaults and a hall called The Cave.
Branik 14°**** 12° Tmavé*** ½

BUDVAR, *České Budĕjovice.* "The original Budweiser", says the English-language export label on the 12° pale beer from the Budvar brewery. The town, Budweis in German, was already supplying beer to the royal court of Bohemia in the early 16th century, although the actual Budvar brewery postdates U.S. Budweiser. The Czech beer has a more emphatic hop character than U.S. Budweiser, but it is still delicate by local standards. It is bigger than the U.S. brew, but by no means fat. The Czech beer has a faint underlying hint of sweetness where the U.S. beer is perhaps fruitier. Both are very firm beers, though the Czech Budvar is more so, and with a cleanness that suggests long lagering. Budvar brewers say they lager for more than three months; U.S. Budweiser gets a minimum of three weeks, which is still more than many U.S. beers. The Czech beer has an alcohol content of about 4.0 percent by weight, 5.0 by volume. The U.S. Budweiser has about 3.8/9 percent by weight, 4.75 by volume. In Prague, Czech Budvar may be enjoyed at a hearty restaurant called U Medvíků, which was itself a brewery in the Middle Ages.
Budvar**** ½
Also recommended: Dalila, a medium-gravity dark lager from the Samson brewery in Česke Budĕjovice.

GAMBRINUS, *Pilsen.* While the original Pilsen lager brewery opened in 1842, the upstart Gambrinus didn't come along until 1869. It has a beer called Světovar that is very similar

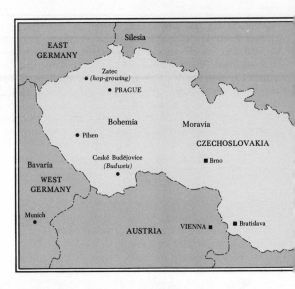

to the true Pilsner and is well made, but without the same individuality of character. The same brewery also has a hoppy, dark, strong lager called Diplomat (6.0% w; 7.5% v).

Svĕtovar*** Diplomat****

MICHALOVCE, *Michalovce.* The early reputation of this brewery derives from its having been established by the great Austrian brewer Anton Dreher, of Vienna. Rather malty, roasty, dark lagers seem to enjoy a particular popularity at the eastern end of the country, and Michalovce has a good example called Širavar.

Širavar***½

Also recommended: Martinský Porter (6.5% w; 8.5% v), the strongest beer in Czechoslavakia.

PILSNER URQUELL, *Pilsen.* The word *Urquell* means original source of, in German, the former language of Bohemia. In the Czech language, the beer is labelled Plzensky Prazdroj. The father of all pilsener-type beers is slightly darker in colour than most of its offspring; Czechs look for what they describe as the "flame" of light refracted in the glass. It should have a good, dense head and, one of its most important characteristics, a delicate and complex but quite definite hop nose. It also has an emphatic hoppiness and dryness in the palate. There is an undertone of something winey or tannic, which probably derives from the use of wooden lagering vessels. Although wooden vessels are always lined with a protective resin, a whole cellar of them probably harbours its own house character nonetheless. Along with the use of fine Saaz hops (though the barley available is not always of the best quality) and a three-month lagering period, this house character further contributes to the individuality of Pilsner Urquell, the beer world's answer to Le Montrachet.

The golden triangle of 19th century brewing science was formed by the Bavarian city of Munich, the Austrian city of Vienna, and the Bohemian town of Pilsen. Today, an overwhelming majority of the world's beers are vague imitations of the Pilsner style. Bohemia, now part of Czechoslovakia, is still famous for its delicate Saaz hops, grown around Žatec, and its Pilsner beer. Budweis and Michelob inspired the great brewer August Busch, of St. Louis, Missouri.

Sadly, Pilsner Urquell doesn't always travel well, partly because the standards of care on the bottling line may not be as high as they should be, perhaps also because of inefficiencies in the handling of exports, and occasionally because the receiving stevedores boycott the product, apparently under the impression that Czechoslovakia is an oppressor nation. If mishandled, the beer easily suffers from oxidation and develops a damp-paper aroma and taste. Pilsner Urquell, which set the standard of 12° Balling (about 4.0% w; 5.0% v) for the style, is available in several famous taverns in Prague. These include U Pinkasů, U zlatého tygra, and U kocoura.

Pilsner Urquell*****

U FLEKŮ, *Prague.* Home-brew house producing a characterful sweetish, dark lager (around 4.3% w; 5.4% v). The beer can be consumed either in the brewery's Gothic cellars, dating back to 1499, or in a garden.

U Fleků****

Also recommended in Prague: the 10° dark lager from Holešovice, and the pale 12° from Staropramen, the biggest of the city's four breweries.

GERMANY

Not only can Germany boast more breweries than any other country, it offers as many as all other nations put together. There are 1,364 breweries in the Federal Republic and another couple of hundred in East Germany, which is a third of the size. As in other countries, closures have taken a terrible toll in recent years, but the number of breweries in Germany should still be the envy of other beer-drinking nations.

How did Germany achieve such preeminence? In part, it is due simply to its geographical position as the biggest nation in northern Europe. With a climate suited to the cultivation of barley, northern Europe was the cradle of brewing, much as the warmer, grape-growing area of southern Europe has for centuries made wine. The Germanic peoples of northern Europe have been brewers since at least Roman times, and without question, beer remains the national drink of both German Republics despite the renown enjoyed by the wines of the Rhine and Mosel.

The reputation of German beers was consolidated by the Bavarian "Purity Law" of 1516, which is today rigidly applied throughout Germany to all beers produced for consumption there, whether they are brewed locally or imported from other countries. The law, known in German as the *Reinheitsgebot*, decrees that the only ingredients that may go into the making of beer are pure water, barley (or wheat in the case of specialty beers), hops, and yeast. Less traditional grains such as corn or rice are not permitted. Nor is sugar. Additives are banned. In the state of Bavaria, the law in its entirety applies also to beers made for consumption in other countries. In other German states, various exemptions are made in the case of beers brewed for export. Not all brewers take advantage of this, and even those who make adjustments to their export products succeed in many cases in producing beers of a higher quality than

are widely found elsewhere in the world. German brewers generally do not pasteurize even their bottled beers if they are intended for local consumption, and a good few even avoid it in their exports.

THE NORTH

No one can be sure why the beers of northern Germany should be especially dry, but it may be significant that, as early as 1101, the city of Hamburg had a famous hop market, to which the precious cones were shipped nearly 180 kilometers (300 miles) down the river Elbe from Bohemia. In the early days, the northerners used hops heavily for their preservative value in beers that were to be dispatched from the region's great ports, either to victual fleets or for export. In either case, a consignment of beer might have to last for some months. The port cities of Hamburg and Bremen were important brewing centers as early as the 15th century, as they are today, even though their names are not immediately associated elsewhere in the world with beer. Then, as now, their position as great exporting cities spread the fame of their products.

Why very dry beers should also be characteristic of that part of the Rhineland closest to the borders of The Netherlands, Belgium, and Luxembourg is even more a matter for speculation, but it is most definitely the case. Of the nine companies that in Germany are classified as "Premium" breweries (broadly, the equivalent of a Grand Cru vineyard), eight are in the north.

BAVARIA-ST. PAULI *Hamburg.* A confusing name, since Bavaria is at the opposite end of Germany from Hamburg. The explanation is that, all over the world and even in Germany, brewers adopted the soubriquet "Bavaria" in the 19th century to indicate that they produced the lager type of beer that Bavaria had made famous. This particular brewery took the name Bavaria in 1897, and gained "St. Pauli" in a merger in 1922. This St. Pauli has nothing to do with the German beer of a similar name marketed in the U.S. by the nearby rival firm of Beck's.

The principal Bavaria-St. Pauli product in the U.S. is Grenzquell, a dry, all-malt beer (3.8% w; 4.75% v). Grenz- quell was originally a product of the famous brewing town of Wernersgrün, in East Germany. Within Germany, Bavaria-St. Pauli's basic products are its Astra beers: ordinary and Premium lagers described respectively as Urtyp and Exclusiv, and a more thin-bodied, drier pil- sener. What makes the company truly notable is a highly distinctive beer from its Premium subsidiary brewery in Jever, Friesland. This product, known simply as Jever Pilsener, has an astonishing 47 units of bitterness. (The legend "herb" on the label is the German word for bitter; it is not an herbal beer, even though its palate is so pronounced as to suggest that it might be). The blander U.S. market beers have bitterness counts as low as 12 or

15, and Jever's (3.9% w; 4.9% v) is less typical of a lager than of a stout. Samplings in other countries can disappoint, because Jever doesn't travel well unless it is handled with proper care. It might be more hardy if it had a longer lagering period than "about four weeks," but its wonderfully hoppy dryness nonetheless ensures its position as a world classic.

Grenzquell*** Astra (range)**½ Jever Pilsener*****

BECK'S, *Bremen.* The biggest exporter of beer from Germany. Before W.W.II, Beck's was something of an international company, but today it brews only in Germany. Its principal product, branded simply as Beck's Bier (4.0% w; 5.0% v), is hard to place stylistically. In its bigness, it is almost southern, but the maltiness is sternly inhibited by a firmness of body, and the final emphasis is on a well-rounded, hoppy bitterness. Beck's also produces an undistinguished Dark (4.0% w; 5.0% v). Similar beers are also produced for the U.S. market under the name St. Pauli Girl. The differences in character between Beck's two brands are not as marked as the similarities, although the St. Pauli beers are perhaps less assertive than those of the Beck brand.

Within Germany, the associate company Haake-Beck serves the local market, and also keeps alive two historically interesting specialties of Bremen. One is a yeasty, sedimented brew known as Kreusenbier, served only in selected taverns. The other, Seefahrtbier, is less of a beer than a malt extract, a reminder of the high-gravity brews produced in ports like Bremen in the past to stock the fleets, then fermented at sea. This is brewed especially for a maritime dinner held each year by the government of Bremen. These traditional products are quite different from today's German beers, and cannot be compared with them.

Beck's Bier***½ Beck's Dark*½ St. Pauli Girl**½
St. Pauli Girl Dark*½

EINBECKER, *Einbeck, Lower Saxony.* Bock beer, today known throughout the world, was born here in Einbeck, and the local brewery still produces an "original" example of the style. Bock is said to have derived its name from a corruption of the last syllable of the name Einbeck. The town, south of Hanover, was a major brewing center in the 13th century, and produced high-gravity beers for export far beyond Germany. Martin Luther is said to have been fortified by Einbeck beer at the Diet of Worms in 1521.

There were once 600 brewers in Einbeck, but today there is only one company, and that is owned by DUB-Schultheiss. Its proud testimony to its heritage is a beer described as Einbecker Ur-Bock. Although the original bock beers would have been top-fermented, and the

Notable Brewing Centers

Map labels:
- BALTIC SEA
- NORTH SEA
- EAST GERMANY
- WEST GERMANY
- Hamburg
- Bremen
- Berlin (*Weisse beers*)
- Hoppy beers
- North Rhine
- Munster (*Altbier*)
- Einbeck (*Bock beers*)
- Dortmund (*"Export" beers*)
- Düsseldorf (*Altbiers*)
- Cologne (*Kölsch beers*)
- Westphalia
- Hoppy Pilsener-type beers
- Rhineland
- Bamberg (*Rauchbiers*)
- Nürnburg
- Stuttgart
- Bavaria (*Weizenbiers*)
- Munich (*pale and dark Münchners, Oktoberfest beers, bock and double bock*)
- ■ Brewing towns
- Brewing regions

modern lager style owes more to the brewers of Munich, the Einbeck product nonetheless has a strong claim to be regarded as a world classic.

Einbecker Ur-Bock*****

FELSENKELLER, *Beerfelden, Hesse.* An excellent example of the countless small German breweries that produce beers of truly excellent quality. Founded in 1782, this little brewery grew out of a guest-house, and remains in private hands. It has in recent years won prizes in Germany for both its full-bodied Export (4.3% w; 5.4% v) and its Pils (4.0% w; 5.0% v), each lagered for three months. A Bock (6.0% w; 7.5% v) is lagered for four months. The name Felsenkeller means rocky cellar, implying the existence of a natural lagering cave. Several other breweries use the same name.

This one, in the happily named town of Beerfelden, is in the Odenwald area, east of Mannheim. There is nothing especially distinctive about these beers, but they are worthy of attention simply for their quality.

Felsen Export***½ Pils***½ Bock***½

HENNINGER, *Frankfurt*. Active internationally, but in fact smaller than its home-town rival, the Binding Brewery. Since Frankfurt does not have a regional brewing style (its local drink is a rather sweet hard cider), neither company can offer anything that is special to the city, but Henninger's products are arguably the more characterful. They include a firm-bodied, dry, pilsener-style beer called Kaiser Pilsner (3.8% w; 4.8% v) and an Export (4.2% w; 5.3%, v), both lagered for between six and nine weeks.

Kaiser Pilsner*** Henninger Export***

HERFORDER, *Herford, Westphalia*. One of the several celebrated producers of pilsener-type beers in the north, and a busy exporter. The company regards its well-rounded Herforder Pils (3.9% w; 4.9% v), lagered for two months, as a Premium product. This is another of the breweries with the corporate name Felsenkeller, but it gives more prominence in its product-identification to the name Herforder, perhaps to avoid confusion with other companies, or possibly because the town has a reputation for beer drinking.

Herforder Pils***

HERRENHAUSEN, *Hanover*. Notably the producer of a well-matured (three months) pilsener-type beer of a marginally higher alcohol content than most (4.1% w; 5.2% v). This presumably leads to its being insultingly labeled as a malt liquor in some states of the U.S., where it also sometimes carries the infantile brand-name Horsy. It is better known simply as Herrenhauser Pilsener.

Herrenhauser Pilsener***½

HOLSTEN, *Hamburg*. Especially well-known in Britain, where its Diät Pils built enormous popularity, initially without any substantial advertising. Diät Pils is a low-carbohydrate beer especially suitable for diabetics, and is not a low-calorie beer for dieters, although many British drinkers believe it to be such. The success of this product has made pils the popular term in Britain for a diet beer, so much so that other breweries feel obliged, when they launch similar products, to present them with the same green foil that identifies Holsten. It happens that Holsten Diät Pils is a well-made beer, adhering in Britain to the German purity law, with the agreeable dryness characteristic of the style, and with an excellent "northern" hoppiness. Beers of this type, being relatively strong (4.8% w; 6.0% v), have a fairly high calorie content.

Exports to Britain of Diät Pils, and of a more conventional lager identified as Export, have substantially helped Holsten's growth, but the company was already one of Germany's biggest brewing groups, with plants in several northern cities. Its subsidiaries include Bergerdorf in Hamburg and Dressler in Bremen, both producing conventional lagers of a typical northern style, but its outstanding product is Moravia-Pils, brewed in Lüheburg. This is a dry, hoppy pilsener-type beer with 38 units of bitterness (3.9% w; 4.9% v).

Holsten Diät Pils**** Moravia-Pils***

LINDENER-GILDE, *Hanover.* Noted for its distinctive top-fermenting specialty, Broyhan Alt, named after the city's great brewmaster of the 16th century. This copper-coloured brew has a wonderfully teasing flirtation of malt and hop in the nose, an assertive, rocky head, and a surprisingly light body (4.2% w; 5.25% v). The company's other products include an excellent and complex beer called Ratskeller Edel-Pils, with 38 units of bitterness and a two-month lagering (4.4% w; 5.5% v).

Broyhan Alt**** Ratskeller Edel-Pils***½

PINKUS MÜLLER, *Münster.* Home-brew beer-house and restaurant famous for its unusually pale, "blonde" version of altbier, occasionally laced with raspberry syrup or even used as the basis for a fruit punch. Despite the diminutive scale of the brewery, its products are exported to the U.S. The highly distinctive Alt (3.9% w; 4.9% v) is dry without being bitter. The tiny brewery produces another top-fermenting beer, a Weizen, as well as a pilsener called Pils. All three products have around the same alcohol content.

Pinkus Alt**** Pinkus Weizen***½ Pinkus Pils**

DORTMUND

The drinker from outside Germany is apt to be confused by the number of beer names that begin with the word Dortmunder. The city of Dortmund has no less than six brewery companies, three or four of which are thoroughly visible in export markets, and all of which proudly preface their names with that of their home town. Things are further confused by the similarity of the names DAB and DUB, which belong to deadly rival breweries. The pride in provenance derives from Dortmund's being the biggest brewing city in Germany as well as in Europe. The Germans themselves hold its beers in high regard, but elsewhere in the world Dortmund lives in the shadow of Munich.

In its output of beer, Dortmund overtook Munich during the industrial growth of the 1920s, though the two cities remain locked in a north-versus-south rivalry. The brewers of Munich can claim that they created several of Germany's famous beer styles, while Dortmund's sole contribution in that respect is the type known, curiously, as Export (4.2% w; 5.2% v). This designation arises from Dortmund's very early emergence as an important brewing city—it was recognized as such as long ago as 1293—and its subsequent development as a center from which beers were "exported" to other parts of Germany. As lager beers from the south gained popularity in the 19th century, Dortmund sought to preserve its own reputation by playing its own distinctive variation on that theme. Lager was first produced in Dortmund in 1843, by the Kronen brewery, but the city's distinctive style was developed by DUB in the 1870s. A Dortmund Export lager was created, drier than those of Munich but less hoppy than that of Pilsen, and slightly stronger than either. Sadly, the distinctive Dortmund Export style has lost ground in recent years. Familiarity has bred contempt, and the beer long favoured by the local miners and steel-workers is thought to be somehow less chic than the pilsener type. Export has, however, held on to more than thirty percent of the market within the city of Dortmund, and still enjoys some popularity in Belgium and The Netherlands. Elsewhere in the world, beers imported from Dortmund usually turn out to be the pilsener type (3.9% w; 4.9% v).

D.A.B. (DORTMUNDER ACTIEN BREWERY) The driest of the Dortmund beers are produced by D.A.B., at the biggest brewery in Germany. Even the company's Dortmunder-style Export is relatively dry, though agreeably rounded. The company more aggressively promotes its surprisingly full-bodied Meister Pils. It has also taken the lead in promoting what it describes as a Dortmund-style Altbier, milder that the classic Düsseldorf brews. In the brewery's name, the word Actien indicates a joint-stock company. The Dortmunder Actien Brewery was founded in 1868, and a century later took over the city's Hansa Brewery, which dates back to 1912. As part of the same consolidation, the two companies became part of the Oetker group.
D.A.B. Export*** Meister Pils** Altbier** ½

DORTMUNDER HANSA. Despite its being part of the D.A.B. group, Hansa retains its own distinct product line. It has a lighter Pils and a rather meatier Export. In its local market, Hansa concentrates on the retail trade. Unlike its big brother, it licenses its beer for production outside of Germany. The first license was granted to the British brewery Cameron's in 1980, but others may follow.
Hansa Export*** Hansa Pils* ½

DORTMUNDER KRONEN. The beers the Dortmunders themselves prefer come from the Kronen brewery, the city's oldest. Within the city limits, Kronen has the biggest share of the market. Although its beers are of outstanding quality, Kronen's local popularity must be helped by the company's long history and the fact that it is still in private hands. Kronen dates back to 1430, and has been owned by the same family since 1729. It has been on its present site since 1873, although the brewery was extensively rebuilt in the 1960s. The brewery is in a neighbourhood called Kronenburg, but seeks to avoid any confusion with the wholly unconnected French company of similar name.

Kronen is very choosy about the varieties of barley it will buy, and has its own maltings. The brewery also has its own spring, yielding the typically soft Dortmund water. With these raw materials, painstaking brewing methods, and a disinclination to pasteurize, Kronen produces malt-accented beers of freshness and flowery delicacy. Its soft, malty Export must be regarded as the definitive example of the style. Its Pilskrone is arguably just too delicate. Fitting between the two styles is a product called Classic (4.1% w; 5.1% v), which was judged to be the best lager in the 1980 International Beer Festival in San Francisco. Kronen beer is available unpasteurized on draught in the U.S. The company ranks fourth in size among the city's brewers.

Dortmunder Kronen Export***** Pilskrone*** Classic***½

DORTMUNDER RITTER. Typical Dortmund beers, on the dry side, sometimes with a slight oiliness, are produced by this, the third in size among the city's breweries. Ritter, partly owned by D.U.B.-Schultheiss, markets its beers with particular success in the nearby industrial towns of the Ruhr valley.

Ritter Export***

DORTMUNDER STIFTS. By far the smallest of the Dortmund breweries, in the south side of the city where it has an extremely local clientele. Stifts produces sweetish beers of good quality. It is part of the group that includes the Carl Funke Stern brewery in Essen; both are owned by the British company Watney.

Stifts Export***½

DORTMUNDER THIER. Malty, full-bodied beers are produced by this privately owned brewery, which ranks fifth in size in the city. Thier's beers are especially popular north of Dortmund, in Westphalian towns like Münster.

Thier Export****

D.U.B. (DORTMUNDER UNION BRAUEREI). The city's second-ranking giant produces carefully balanced beers. Its Export is rescued from blandness by underlying hints of fruitiness. Its Siegel Pils has a good hop dryness but with relatively low bitterness. This company has a beer called Brinckhoff's Number 1, named after its first brewmaster and in the style of Kronen Classic. D.U.B. was founded in 1873 as the result of the union of ten or a dozen local breweries. Exactly 100 years later, it formed a group with the Schultheiss brewery of Berlin and others.

D.U.B. Export*** Siegel Pils*** Brinckhoff's No. 1**

DÜSSELDORF

For the discriminating drinker, Düsseldorf is the most emphatically different of German cities in that its highly distinctive style of beer is universally served and widely preferred by the local people. Brewers in some other cities in north Germany have stuck to the old top-fermentation method, and it is perhaps understandable in the light of history that the Rhineland clung to customs that differed from the practices of Prussia and Bavaria, but the Düsseldorfers seem to be the most determinedly traditionalist of all.

The old, or *alt*, beers of Düsseldorf have a rich copper colour, and are superficially very similar to English ales. However, they have a rounder, cleaner palate deriving both from the use of single-cell pure yeast cultures and three to six weeks of cold conditioning. They generally have a starting gravity of 12° to 12.5° Plato (1048–1050 British, 3.5% w; 4.4% v) and emerge with a soft, fullish body despite a fermentation that customarily verges on the violent. The Hallertau hops widely used in German brewing are often augmented with, or replaced by, Spalt hops.

The best way to sample the style is direct from the cask, in unpasteurized form, in one of the city's four home-brew houses. At each of these, it is possible simply to have a few beers in the typical small cylindrical glasses, or to enjoy an inexpensive but hefty German meal of sausages, smoked meats, and sauerkraut at a scrubbed table.

Even the altbier of the large breweries is often served straight from the cask, without pressure, and is generally not pasteurized. Altbier is, however, always filtered. Among the major names, Hannen is the most widely available. Hannen Alt is very well made, a soft, rounded, delicately balanced brew. The popular Diebels is firm-bodied. Frankenheim Alt is hoppy but rather thin, Schlösser on the sweet side, Düssel Alt (Hirsch) fruity with plenty of character, and Rhenania a little grainy.

Although all of these are very well worth sampling, the visiting beer-drinker will want to taste altbier fresh from the craftsman's cellar. With the exception of Schumacher, which is in the city center, all four of the

Düsseldorf home-brew houses are in the Altstadt (old town). In two, Zum Schlüssel and Zum Uerige, the brewery can be seen from the drinking and dining area. In all four, a seasonal strong altbier (around 6.0% w; 7.5% v) is produced in March and September. This is variously known as a Latzenbier or Sticke Alt.

FERDINAND SCHUMACHER, *Oststrasse*. Although the home-brew houses don't differ greatly, this is the most refined in tone, and its altbier is the palest in colour, lightest in palate, and maltiest, but of excellent quality. The beer is also available in the Goldene Kessel, in Bolkerstrasse in the old town, and at the Neue Kessel, near the Frankenheim brewery. Visitors to Bolkerstrasse might care to know that Heinrich Heine was born there, on the site of what is now the Hühner Hugo restaurant.

Schumacher Altbier****

IM FÜCHSCHEN, *Ratingerstrasse*. As famous for its food, especially its *eisbein*, as for its Altbier, which is delightfully hoppy without being acidic. The beer is subtly balanced to combine a dryness with a full, firm body.

Im Füchschen Altbier****

ZUM SCHLÜSSEL, *Bolkerstrasse*. Among the altbiers, the bitter but light and slightly acidic example produced at Zum Schlüssel is the one in which the hint of a family resemblance to English ale can be most readily detected. Although Zum Schlüssel is genuinely a home-brew house, it has grown beyond its original status. The company, established in 1936, expanded in 1963 by opening a second, free-standing brewery under the name of Gatzweiler that has since grown to become a major commercial producer of altbier. Gatzweiler and Zum Schlüssel altbiers are similar in palate.

Zum Schlüssel/Gatzweiler Alt***½

ZUM UERIGE, *Bergerstrasse*. A rambling old house producing a superb Altbier with a big, earthy hop aroma, assertive bitterness, and yeasty depth. Excellent food, too—Zum Uerige even has its own butcher.

Zum Uerige Altbier*****

COLOGNE

So proud is the city of Cologne to have its own beer style that its brewers have gone to the law to protect the exclusive identity of their product. In the German language, the city is called Köln, and its beer is described as kölschbier or, commonly, just kölsch. Only in Cologne and the adjoining metropolitan area may brewers produce a beer of this description.

The beer style of Cologne is most unusual. Top-fermentation is always used, but the beers are as light in colour as a pilsener. They are (by German standards although not by British), low in carbonation, with a very faintly lactic sourness in the nose, and a full but subtle hop palate. Although hops are by nature both dry and bittering, these characteristics manifest themselves in kölsch in a restrained fashion. In body, kölsch is light and refreshing, promoting the appetite while, in advance, aiding the dilgestion. It is, among beers, what a delicate, dry, flowery Italian vermouth, with a swoosh of soda, is to the world of wines. The Germans regard kölsch very much in this way, as an aperitif to be drunk with bar snacks.

Its original gravity is usually around 12° Plato (1048 British, about 3.7% w; 4.6% v). Kölsch is such a subtle beer that the differences between the products of the ten or so specialist brewers are by no means pronounced, but, like the altbier of Düsseldorf, it is at its freshest and most expressive when sampled straight from the cask in a home-brew house. As in Düsseldorf, the beer is filtered, but not pasteurized, after maturation, and the casks are made of wood.

Across the road from Cologne's magnificent Gothic cathedral is a tavern called the Cölner Höfbrau but better known by its business name of P.J. Früh, at which kölsch may be sampled in the traditional manner. The beer is brought to the table by waiters in their customary uniform of blue pullovers and leather aprons. The waiters are known colloquially as Kobes, which is believed to be a familiar contraction of Jakob.

With a kölsch or two, in the characteristically tall, narrow, cylindrical glasses, the almost mandatory snack is "half a hen", which turns out for reasons of impenetrably German whimsy to mean a wedge of cheese with a roll. Or "Cologne caviare", which is a type of blood sausage. Or mettwurst, of the steak tartare type, served with lots of onions.

At P.J. Früh, the biggest of the several drinking and dining rooms was originally the brewhouse. The tavern is still supplied from its own brewery, but not within the building. A short walk away, the tiny Sion brewery has its own tavern in Unter Taschenmacher. An even smaller brewery, Päffgen, of Friesenstrasse, produces kölsch solely for its own tavern. Kölsch is not always easy to find beyond the Rhineland, and the only brand widely exported is Küppers.

MUNICH AND BAVARIA

The state of Bavaria and its greatest city, Munich, are at the root of German brewing tradition, and there are solid foundations beneath the beer culture of this part of Germany. About two thirds of the breweries in Germany are in this state. Next door, the other great southern state, Baden-Württemberg, is the second most populous in breweries. Although there are some big names among the brewers of the south, the majority of its beers come from tiny craft companies in small towns and villages.

Even more significant than the profusion of breweries is the number of beer styles that originate in the south: the Münchner pale and dark types, the Märzenbier or Oktoberfest types (taken from Vienna and further nurtured), the modern bottom-fermenting version of bock, double bock, and weizenbier (also sometimes known as weissbier). No other single region of Germany, or of any country, can match this contribution.

It is odd that all but the last of these styles are malt-accented, when one of the reasons for Bavaria's growth as a brewing region must have been its long history of hop cultivation. Germany is the world's largest producer of hops, and most of them are grown in Bavaria, in districts like Hallertau, Spalt, and Tettnang. (These three growing areas are stylistically very important, as are Bohemia in Czechoslovakia and Kent in England).

The success of Bavarian brewing also owes something to politics; over the centuries the rulers of the region have protected and developed the industry. The most important single act was the purity law passed by the Elector of Bavaria in 1516, but the Prime Minister of Bavaria and the members of his Cabinet still take part in a number of state ceremonies to usher in the various seasonal beers each year.

From the pre-Lenten carnival in February, to the double bock season around St. Joseph's Day (March 19), to the May bock receptions, the Oktoberfest, and finally the season of extra-strong Christmas beers, the drinker in Bavaria has barely a quiet month. Nor, with the famous beer gardens and halls, does he have a shortage of temples at which to worship. (A beer garden is often known as a keller in German, but this implies merely that the casks are kept in a cellar, not that they are consumed in subterranean conditions.) When people in other countries try to recreate a German bierkeller, what they are imitating is a beer hall. The big brewers of Munich and other major Bavarian cities have both beer halls and beer gardens, each often seating drinkers by the thousands, and there are beer gardens throughout the Danube valley and in the foothills of the Alps.

ANDECHS, *Erling-Andechs, Bavaria.* No doubt the inspiration for the U.S. Andeker brand, but exactly when or how is lost in the mists of history. German Kloster Andecher beers are made at a monastery (hence the name: *kloster* means cloister). They may well be the maltiest beers in the world. When a bock beer from Andechs is poured, the room fills with the fresh, heavy aroma of malt. It is truly a beer with the aroma of the brewhouse. Such delights, as well as ecclesiastical schnapps, can be sampled in the beer garden at the brewery, southwest of Munich. Other renowned religious establishments in Bavaria include the monastery of Ettal, Oberammergau, and the convent brewery of Mallersdorf, which is run by a nun.

Bergbock Hell**** Bergbock Dunkel****
Doppelbock Hell**** Doppelbock Dunkel****

AUGUSTINER, *Munich.* The oldest established brewery in Munich, founded in the 14th century, originally as part of a monastery. Its beers are greatly favoured by the people of Munich, and its adjoining beer garden, the Augustiner-keller, is perhaps the least touristic in the city. Augustiner beer is also served at the 7,000-seat Hirschgarten, near the Nymphenburg Castle. The brewery produces a particularly good example of the dark Münchner style, and an excellent double bock called Maximator.

Augustiner Dunkel**** Maximator***½

AYING, *Aying, Bavaria.* The best-known "village brewery" in Bavaria. The village comprises nothing more than a brewery, a beer garden, a tavern, a church (with the typical onion-shaped tower), a marketplace, and a few farmhouses. The malty, clean-tasting beers of the Aying brewery can be tasted in Munich at a tavern on the Platzl. The brewery's Platzl Spezial is a sweetish, full-bodied pale beer (around 4.0% w; 5.0% v). It also produces an excellent bock called Andreas.

Platzl Spezial**** Andreas Bock***½

DINKELACKER, *Stuttgart.* A major brewing company that also has the distinctive Sanwald wheat beers. Dinkelacker has a considerable range of products, among which a special export version of its CD Pils is readily available in the U.S. This is a firm-bodied beer of (4.2% w; 5.3% v) brewed according to the purity law, lagered for seven or eight weeks, and unpasteurized. The local Stuttgart version is a couple of decimal points lower in alcohol and has ten days' less lagering since its stability is less of a factor. Although both are on the sweet side for a pils, the local version is markedly the hoppier of the two. The Sanwald label has an altbier, and a diät lager, but its principal product is its Weizen Krone wheat beer at (4.1% w; 5.1% v).

CD Pils (export)*** (domestic)*** Sanwald Weizen Krone****

E.K.U., *Kulmbach, Bavaria.* The second strongest beer in the world, aptly named Kulminator, is produced by the Erste Kulmbacher brewery, better known simply as E.K.U., just north of Bayreuth. The brewery has a full range of beers, including two that bear the name Kulminator. One of these, additionally identified as Dunkles Starkbier (dark, strong), is a standard double bock (6.0% w; 7.6% v). As if that were not a sufficiently respectable strength, the brewery then ascends to its Kulminator Urtyp Hell (original, pale), with the figure 28 prominent on the label. The figure indicates the original gravity in degrees Plato (9.8% w; 12.4% v). This brew is lagered for nine months, and undergoes an unusual freezing process in which its strength is concentrated by the removal of watery ice. Devotees of German eiswein might like to try an eisbock. The beer is very heavy, with its rich maltiness offset only by some fruity esters and the alcohol. It bears only occasional drinking and is hardly subtle, but must be regarded as a classic on the grounds of its potency.

Kulminator Dunkles Starkbier****
Kulminator 28 Urtyp Hell*****

FEUERFEST, *Treuchtlingen, Bavaria.* Guaranteed to have been lagered for at least a year, extremely strong (8.8% w; 11.0% v), and understandably inclined to be expensive, Feuer-Fest Edel Bier is a minor classic from this very small Bavarian brewery. The allusion to fire (feuer) derives from the way in which the copper is heated. FeuerFest is very much a hand-made beer and is presented in numbered and sealed bottles, which make it look less like a beer than a Cognac. It has a rich character reminiscent of plums in brandy, though the brewers promote it as an aperitif. It is labeled only with the brand name and is most readily identified in that way, although the brewing company is actually called Schäffbräu.

FeuerFest Edel Bier****

FÜRSTENBERG, *Donaueschingen, Baden.* The noble family of Fürstenberg has owned this brewery in the Black Forest since it was founded by the Duke of Freiburg in the 13th century. It is now a sizable concern, classified as a Premium brewery, and exporting to several parts of the world. In the U. S., its basic brand of beer, brewed under the purity law and bottled in Germany, is imported by Pabst. The beer (around 4.0% w; 5.0% v) is lagered for a minimum of nine weeks, and is flash-pasteurized. It is firm-bodied, and clean-tasting, with a slight malt emphasis.

Fürstenberg***½

HACKER-PSCHORR, *Munich.* One of the major Munich brewers (the others being Augustiner, H.B., Löwenbräu, Spaten, and Paulaner). Hacker-Pschorr has no particular specialty, but all of its products are sturdy examples of Munich's brewing tradition and the company takes particular pride in its double bock, which is called Animator.

Animator****

H.B. (HOFBRÄUHAUS), *Munich.* The royal brewery of Bavaria, now owned by the State, and famous for its bock beer. The brewery was founded by the Duke of Bavaria in 1589, and in 1610 it adopted and popularized the strong bock style of beer that had originated in Einbock, in Lower Saxony. The Hofbräuhaus has been so central to the attentions of the Munich people that when prices of beer were raised in 1848, the subsequent outcry obliged the King, Ludwig I, to abdicate. The Hofbräuhaus beer hall, on the Platzl, has had its moments of notoriety but it remains, as H.L. Mencken put it, "the Parthenon of beer-drinking"; and on May Day, the Prime Minister of Bavaria and the Mayor of Munich are customarily there to witness the tapping of the first cask of the new season's bock.

Though history demands that it share the honours with Einbeck's product, the fine Hofbräuhaus Maibock is without question a world classic. The brewery is also credited with having popularized another beer from foreign parts—weizenbier, which had its origins in Bohemia. H.B.'s fine version is called Edel-Weizen. In much the way that weizenbier is served with a slice of lemon, so Maibock is best sampled with a side order of a lemon-tinged, parsley-flavoured sausage called weiss-wurst. This white sausage, taken with a sweet mustard, is eaten only in the mornings.

Maibock***** Edel-Weizen*****

KAISERDOM, *Bamberg, Bavaria.* "Smoked" beer, rauchbier in German, is the extraordinary specialty of the baroque town of Bamberg, between Bayreuth and Wurzburg. Outside Germany, Kaiserdom Rauchbier is probably the easist to find. Although the Kaiserdom brewery produces a full range of more conventional beers, it does regard its Rauchbier as something of a specialty. The intensely smoky palate derives from the kilning of the malt over a fire of beechwood logs. Historically, all malts for brewing were dried by direct fire, but the particular character imparted by the beech of the Franconian woods, and perhaps the palates thus bred into local drinkers, led this relatively isolated town to persist with the old method until its beers became a prized specialty.

Acquired tastes are, by definition, worthy of cultivation, and that is true of Rauchbier. As an aperitif, it is a natural accompaniment to the great smoked hams of Bavaria, and its admirers in the U.S. have been known to enjoy it for Sunday brunch with bagels and lox. On its own, it is to beer what the Islay malts are to whisky. Kaiserdom Rauchbier starts from a relatively high original gravity of 13.80° Plato (1055 British), and emerges at 4.2 percent w; 5.25 v. Like all rauchbiers, it is bottom-fermented, and it is lagered for three months.

Kaiserdom Rauchbier****½

KULMBACHER MÖNSCHOF, *Kulmbach, Bavaria.* In the same town as E.K.U. (of Kulminator renown), and a rival, this brewery is very well regarded, with its own specialties. Its basic brew is a full-bodied, Bavarian-style helles called Maingold (4.27% w; 5.3% v) that is lagered for six to eight weeks, but its monastic origins are reflected in a couple of specialties. One is a "monastic dark" called Kloster Schwarz, which is full in body but intentionally modest in strength (3.97% w, 4.9% v) and lagered for six to eight weeks. The other is a malty "dark cloister bock" called Klosterbock Dunkel (5.12% w; 6.4% v), that is lagered for three months and in which the profundity of color is again a striking characteristic.

Maingold***½ Kloster Schwarz***½
Klosterbock Dunkel****

LÖWENBRÄU, *Munich.* Of the Munich brewers, Löwenbräu is by far the best known outside Germany. Within its home country, state, and city, it does not have any special renown. Löwenbräu's reputation was not helped when, some years ago, the company mooted the idea that the purity law should be waived for exports. Other parts of Germany may permit that to some degree, but Bavaria still doesn't. The subsequent licensing of Miller in the U.S. to produce a "Löwenbräu" beer rather different from anything brewed in Munich has also been a mixed blessing for the reputations concerned. Perhaps to the confusion of U.S. visitors, there is no single Löwenbräu beer in Munich. Like all of the city's brewers, the company produces a range of different products. Among them, one of the more interesting is Löwenbräu's example of sedimented wheat beer, Hefeweizen. Further confusion arises because there is more than one brewing company called Löwenbräu. The one in Munich is by far the largest, but the name has been used in one form or another by at least a score of unconnected breweries in the German-speaking world, including a well-respected small firm in Zürich, Switzerland. After all, Löwenbräuerei simply means "Lion Brewery" and there are plenty of those even in the English-speaking world.

Löwenbräu Hefeweizen***½

PAULANER, *Munich.* A world classic among breweries. The world has Paulaner to thank for the magnificent double bock beers of Germany. The brewery is also one of two claimants (the other is Spaten) to the distinction of having produced the first Munich-style pale lager. The double bock named Salvator, after the Saviour, has its origins in a strong beer produced by the monks of St. Francis of Paula during the late 18th century. The monks, who originally came from Italy during the Counter-Reformation, lost their brewery in the Napoleonic period, but it continued to operate as a commercial business, eventually growing into today's large concern, Paulaner-Salvator-Thomasbräu. The Paulaner pale beer was introduced in 1928. Today, Paulaner has two pale beers. Like all of the everyday session beers in this big-drinking city, the basic Münchner Hell has a modest alcohol content (3.8% w; 4.8% v) which is typical of a U.S. premium beer. The "original" pale, Paulaner Urtyp (4.3% w; 5.5% v) is lagered for eight or nine weeks. Salvator (5.87% w; 7.51% v) is lagered for ten weeks. It has an impeccably balanced palate, and a well-rounded body. The brewery has ten principal products in all, including a couple of "old Bavarian" (altbayerisches) wheat beers. One of these, Hefe-Weissbier (4.04% w; 5.17% v) is yeast-sedimented and bottle-fermented.

Munchner Hell**** Urtyp***** Salvator*****
Hefe-Weissbier***½

RIEGELE, *Augsburg*. The people of the handsome city of Augsburg are known for their appetite for typical Swabian regional noodle dishes, and have some fine beers with which to accompany them. The Augsburger brewery of Riegele, for example, produces a dozen different styles, including a well-matured pale wheat beer called Perlweizen and a sedimented Hefeweizen (both 4.0% w; 5.0% v). At a similar strength, the brewery also has an excellent, typically Bavarian, malty lager called Spezi. There is a slightly stronger (4.4% w; 5.5% v) Christmas beer that is even meatier, a beautifully mature dark Münchner, Dunkel Spezial, (around 4.5% w; 5.6% v), and an excellent double bock called Speziator (around 6.3% w; 7.9% v) that is lagered for three months.

Perlweizen*** Hefeweizen***½ Spezi****
Weihnachts Christmas beer**** Dunkel Spezial****
Speziator****

SCHLENKERLA, *Bamberg*. Smoked beer is the sole product of this tavern brewery, which traces its history back to 1678. By virtue of such specialization, its product might claim to be the classic example of this style. It is in any case the most intense of the Bamberg smoked beers, with an almost aggressive character. In the number of brews that it embraces, rauchbier is a minor style, but it most emphatically should not be written off as a curiosity. Not only in their history but also in their character, these are utterly magnificent beers. The products of the Heller-Trum Schlenkerla brewery, those of Wörner Bürgerbräu Kaiserdom, and others in Bamberg should be cherished.

Schlenkerla's classic, which the brewery additionally qualifies, rather confusingly, as being a Märzenbier (perhaps because of a highish gravity of 13.4° Plato) is full-bodied (3.6% w; 4.5% v) and is lagered for two months.

Schlenkerla Märzen*****

SCHNEIDER, *Munich*. A small, family brewery that is easily overlooked among its giant neighbours in Munich. Schneider has a full range of beers, but specializes in wheat brews, among which its dark, strong Aventinus (6.5% w; 7.8% v) is especially interesting.

Aventinus****½

SPATEN, *Munich*. The most significant brewery in the world in the development of the beers that are drunk in most nations today. The Spaten brewery was not so much the birthplace of modern lager-brewing as the scene of its conception. Spaten gave the world perhaps the greatest brewer ever, Gabriel Sedlmayr II, whose work, collaboration, and teachings seem to have paved the way for the production, by Dreher, of the first modern lager beer, in Vienna in 1841, the perfection of the method in Pilsen, and the popularization of the style by Carlsberg of Copenhagen. Lager-brewing had existed before then, but by empirical and unreliable methods. Sedlmayr cultivated the first dependable lager yeast, and his brewery was later a pioneer in the use of refrigeration (Linde built his first machine in 1873, at the Spaten brewery) and steam heating (1876).

The first Munich lager was dark in colour, and gave rise to the international use of the term Münchner to describe a beer of that style. Spaten's dark lager, Dunkel Export (4.0% w; 5.0% v), might thus be regarded as the classic example of the style. It is lagered for eight weeks, and is malty in both the nose and the palate. A second classic beer style was popularized with the introduction in 1872, by Sedlmayr's brother Josef of a Vienna-style Märzenbier for Oktoberfest. Today, Spaten proclaims its originality in the name Ur-Märzen (4.4% w; 5.58% v) a beer that is lagered for fourteen weeks, and emerges with an immensely dexterous balance between maltiness and hop character. A third innovation was the introduction, in 1894, of what was described at the time as a pilsener-type pale beer.

Today, Spaten has a very hoppy Pils (4.0% w; 5.0% v) that is lagered for fourteen weeks. It also has a Munich-style pale beer, Munchner Hell (3.7% w; 4.6% v) that is a little hoppier than most examples of the style, and is lagered for six weeks. Like some of its contemporaries, Spaten also has an Export-style pale beer called Spatengold (4.3% w; 5.4% v) lagered for eight weeks. Its bock is also pale, and is named Franziskus after the one-time Franciscan monastery brewery that was for many decades run by Joseph Sedlmayr. Franziskus (5.3% w; 6.7% v) is surprisingly hoppy. Spaten's double bock, which is dark, is called Optimator (5.4% w; 6.8% v). Both are lagered for eight weeks. The brewery also has two wheat beers (4.1% w; 5.2% v), a sparkling Club-Weisse, and a sedimented Hefeweiss-bier. Spaten's beers are, in general, hoppier than those of some rivals, and the brewery's lagering times are shorter than those employed in some houses, but its range gives an excellent indication of the styles of beer typically found in Bavaria.

Dunkel Export***** Ur-Märzen***** Spaten Pils***½
Münchner Hell**** Spatengold*** Franziskus****
Optimator***½ Club-Weisse***½ Hefeweissbier****

TUCHER, *Nürnberg*. An astonishingly dry double-hopped beer called simply Tucher Doppelhopfen, is the specialty product of this brewery, which produes a full range of types, all very well made. The Doppelhopfen carries on the label a guarantee of three months of lagering time, and all the beers bear a similar assurance that they adhere to the purity law.

Tucher Doppelhopfen****

WEIHENSTEPHAN, *Freising, Bavaria*. Described as the oldest brewery in the world. The Benedictines cultivated hops in Weihenstephan as early as 768, and commercial brew-ing has been going on there since 1040. The present-day brewery is linked with the State Hofbräufhaus in nearby Munich. There is also in Weihenstephan one of the world's leading institutes for the study of brewing, which is part of the Technical University of Munich. The insti-tute and the brewery cooperate with each other. The brewery produces an outstanding range of wheat beers, which are characteristically lively, and among which a Weizenbock (5.3% w; 6.6% v) is a classic example of the style. There are several other small breweries in this area specializing in wheat beers, and all produce excellent products.

Weihenstephan Weizenbock*****

WÜRZBURGER HOFBRÄU, *Würzburg*. The important city of Würzburg, in the Franconian region of Bavaria, is better known internationally for its wines. The dry Sylvaner steinwein stands apart from other German white wines both geographically and stylistically. So important has wine been to Würzburg that in 1434 the city fathers tried to ban beer by forbidding brewing forever. Like King Canute, they could not stem the tide; in Bavaria, wine was to become secondary to beer, although Franconia now has the best of both worlds. By 1643, Würzburg had a Hofbräuhaus, and still does. Würzburger Hofbräu pro-duces typically full-bodied Bavarian beers, although they are less malty than some. After early exports to the U.S.

performed very well in blindfold tastings, the brewery entered into a major deal with Anheuser-Busch to export German-brewed beer to be bottled in the U.S. The beer brewed for the U.S. market is of German quality but slightly lighter in body than the basic Würzburger Hofbräu beer in the local market. Würzburger's wide range of other products includes an excellent Oktoberfest beer that is exported to the U.S.

Würzburger Hofbräu (Germany)*** ½
Würzburger (U.S.) ***Oktoberfest*** ½

BERLIN

Napoleon's troops are said to have accorded the soubriquet "le Champagne du Nord" to Berliner weisse beer. The Prussians have preferred wheat beer ever since Frederick the Great trained as a brewer, and it remains a proud regional style in Berlin on both sides of the Wall.

Berliner weisse is altogether different from the wheat beers of south Germany, which are made from a mash containing at least half wheat malt, and sometimes two thirds; Berliner weisse employs only a quarter. The southern wheat beers usually have a fairly conventional alcohol content (4.0% w; 5.0% v) and some are stronger still; Berliner weisse is intentionally low in alcohol (about 2.5% w; 3.0% v) and is served as a refreshing summer drink. Most important of all, Berliner weisse is made more quenching by a lactic acid fermentation induced by the addition of a sour milk culture. The beer is then conditioned in the bottle.

If the beer is poured carelessly, so that sediment enters the glass, the epithet *weisse* (white) begins to attain a meaning, but this is not the way to do it. Berliner weisse is customarily served with a lacing of raspberry syrup or essence of woodruff. It is the Buck's Fizz of the beer world, and is even served in a big, bowl-shaped glass like an overgrown Champagne saucer.

Berliner weisse is one of the world's classic styles, enjoyed throughout Germany in the summer and widely brewed in the U.S. until Prohibition. The two great Berlin breweries, Schultheiss and Kindl, each have their own version. The former has an apple-like bouquet, is very dry, and extremely refreshing, but the latter is arguably the more uncompromising in its sourness.

Kindel Berliner Weisse*****
Schultheiss Berliner Weisse****

SCANDINAVIA

The reputation for beer that attaches to Scandinavia as a whole may derive in part from images of thirsty Vikings, but in modern times it has deep foundations specifically in one country, Denmark. The founder of the Carlsberg company, of Copenhagen, Denmark spread the popularity of lager-brewing after after he brought a supply of bottom-fermenting yeast by stage-coach from Munich, a journey of 500 miles, in 1845–46. This led eventually to the isolation, in Copenhagen, of the first single-cell culture, in honor of which bottom-fermenting beer yeasts the world over are known as *Saccharomyces carlsbergensis*. Denmark remains a major brewing nation, although its industry is domi-nated by one group, and its beers are inclined to blandness.

The other two Scandinavian countries, Norway and Sweden, together with Finland (not strictly speaking part of Scandinavia) have vigorous traditions of home-brewing in agricultural communities. These traditions, which date back to the earliest knowledge of brewing in Western Europe, have embraced ingredients that pre-date the hop, such as alder twigs, angelica, honey, and especially juniper berries. These ingredients are fea-tured in special beers made by commercial brewers. Notable examples are the Spetsat herb beer and Rodeorm Mead from Sweden's Till brewery.

Both Denmark and Norway have specialty beers of the malt-extract type, but apart from those, the brewers of the North produce primarily conventional lagers, including the occasional bock. A typical brewery's range of products is likely to be wider in Denmark than in the other countries. One curiosity is the survival of Imperial Stouts, which have at least a tenuous relationship with the beer trade that existed between Western Europe and the Tsarist Empire in the 18th and 19th centuries. Among these, only the Finnish example is truly top-fermented, but they are all excellent and robust beers.

In quality, the beers of Norway are brewed in ad-herence to the German purity law, but that is not applied to exports. A similar ordinance in Finland has been diluted to the point where it no longer means a great deal.

The drinker can have an enjoyable time in Denmark, but in the other Nordic countries, and especially Iceland, he is fenced in by temperance restrictions that affect the strength, variety, and availability of beer. As a consequence, drinking is less fun and often more determinedly intense than it might otherwise be.

AASS, *Drammen, Norway.* The name Aass is, in Norwegian at least, pronounced rather like *horse* without the *h*. Aass is one of about a dozen small brewing companies in Norway, but it offers a slightly more interesting range than some of them, and its catchy name has spread to the U.S. through exports of its very agreeable, dryish, smoky Bock (4.9% w; 6.4% v). Most Norwegian beers are on the dry side, firm and clean. The rest of the Aass range comprises a pale pilsener-type and a dark Bavarian (both 3.5% w; 4.5% v), a pale Export (4.5% w; 5.7% v) and an excellent Christmas beer (4.6% w; 6.0% v). The Norwegian name for a Christmas beer sounds, for etymological reasons, remarkably like "Yule Ale" although it is rendered as Jule Øl. The word ale is derived from the Norse, but øl (in Swedish, öl; in Finnish, olut) simply means beer, and does not imply top-fermentation.
Bok (Bock)***½ Pilsner*** Bayer (Bavarian)*** Export*** Jule****

ALBANI, *Odense, Denmark.* In the town where Hans Christian Andersen was born, and a possible source of his inspiration. There are about fifteen small brewing companies in Denmark, and Albani is one of the more interesting. It has several impressive products, among them a strong Giraf lager (5.4% w; 6.75% v), an Easter brew called Påske Bryg (6.2% w; 7.75% v), and an imperial-style Porter (5.7% w; 7.1% v) all noteworthy.
Giraf***½ Påske Bryg***½ Porter****

CARLSBERG, *Copenhagen, Denmark.* The strange adventure that gave birth to Carlsberg (see p. 48) begat an extraordinary company as well as a famous beer. Carlsberg is not only a brewery but also a charity. All of its profits go to the pursuit of the arts and sciences, not only in Denmark but all over the world, through foundations set up by the father and son who founded the company. Carlsberg continues to operate as a philanthropic organization despite now being only one part of a larger group, United Breweries. This group includes another famous name, Tuborg, as well as the smaller Danish breweries Neptun and Wiibroes.

While it is true that the single most important factor in the palate of all beers is probably the yeast strain used, it is appropriate that this should be so evident in the case of Carlsberg. Like all brewers who have plants in different places and various licensing agreements, Carlsberg sees the universal use of the same yeast as absolutely essential to continuity of character. Among brewers who produce and market their beers in many different countries, Carlsberg is considered in the industry to be the most exacting about the standards to be maintained, although the actual range of brands is always selected to suit what are considered to be the local requirements, especially with respect to alcohol content. Because Carlsberg gives the appearance of being monolithic, drinkers outside Denmark are not generally aware of how many different brands the company produces. In Denmark, Carlsberg markets a dozen beers, representing a permutation of four styles (Pilsener, Vienna, Münchner, Stout) across five categories of alcoholic strength. A further six versions of Carlsberg beers are produced in Denmark for specific export markets in Europe. These include all-malt beers for Germany; for most markets, including Denmark, Carlsberg uses a proportion of corn grits. Outside Denmark, two dozen Carlsberg products are brewed in a dozen countries. In Britain, Malawi, and Malaysia, Carlsberg has participated in the creation of local companies. In a number of other countries, though not the U.S., its products are brewed under license. In Canada, for example, they are produced by Carling.

The defining characteristic of the principal Carlsberg beers is a roundness and mildness, underpinned by some fruitiness, that is almost a style in itself; they are hardly true Pilseners. In Britain, the company's basic brew is Carlsberg Pilsner Lager (about 2.6% w; 3.2% v), and what might be regarded internationally as the basic Carlsberg (3.7% w; 4.6% v) is known as Hof. The company also exports Gold Label (4.0–4.5% w; 5.0–5.6% v), as well as Carlsberg 68 to Britain and Elephant to the U.S. (both 5.5–5.7% w; 6.8–7.1% v) and Carlsberg Special (6.8% w; 8.5% v). Carlsberg also makes an excellent Imperial Stout, also labelled as Gammel (meaning old) Porter (6.1% w; 7.6% v).

Carlsberg Pilsner (Britain) * ½ Carlsberg (International)** ½
Gold Label*** 68*** ½ Elephant*** ½ Special****
Imperial Stout**** ½

CERES, *Aarhus, Denmark.* Far smaller than the Carlsberg-Tuborg grouping, but the second-largest brewing enterprise in Denmark nonetheless, with plants in several towns. An interesting range of products includes a tasty imperial-style Stout (6.0% w; 7.5% v). A bizarre but colourful beer called Red Eric is no longer produced.

Ceres Danish Stout****

FAXE, *Fakse, Denmark.* "Purveyors of beer to the Danish people" is how this independently minded brewery describes itself, taking a proletarian side-swipe at the Carlsberg-Tuborg grouping's pride in supplying the Royal

Family. In a similar spirit, Faxe refused to use a standard returnable bottle adopted by the rest of the industry in the 1970s. While almost all Danish beers are pasteurized, a celebrated brand called Faxe Fad isn't, and the brewery considers that, for this reason, it requires a stronger, darker bottle to guard against explosion and light. Although the product is bottled, the word Fad means draught. In several parts of the world, brewers have produced packaged brands labeled as draught to indicate that they like tap beers, are unpasteurized. Faxe Fad (3.6% w; 4.5% v) has a notably fresh, clean taste, with the mildness characteristic of Danish beers. A stronger Faxe Danish Beer (4.5% w; 5.6% v) is exported unpasteurized in the can, but pasteurized in the bottle.

Faxe Fad***½ Faxe Danish Beer***½

KOFF, *Helsinki, Finland.* Noted for its genuinely top-fermented Imperial Stout, also known in the local market as Porter (5.6% w; 7.0% v). This outstanding beer is firm, quite dry, pleasantly roasty, and satisfying. The brewery also produces a conventional lager labeled as Koff Finnish Beer. (4.3% w; 5.4% v), which is quite big, and dryish without being especially bitter.

Finnish beers are characteristically firm, clean and fairly dry, and the law demands that no more than 20 percent of adjuncts are used. The word Koff is an abbreviation of Sinebrychoff, the name of the Russian who founded the brewery in 1819 when Finland was part of the Russian Empire. Sinebrychoff is the second-largest brewery in Finland. The largest is Hartwall, and the third is Mallasjuoma, which at one point exported a product called Finlandia, but that brand has now been withdrawn. Beyond those three, there remain only two small breweries, Lapin and Pyynikki.

Koff Imperial Stout****½ Koff Finnish Beer***

LOLLAND-FALSTERS, *Nykøbing, Denmark.* A folksy, small brewery producing typically Danish mild lagers, with a house style that is slightly maltier than most, and very fresh and clean. The basic product is a pilsener-style beer (3.6% w; 4.5% v).

Lolland-Falsters Pilsener***

POLAR BEER, *Reykjavik, Iceland.* The beer of Iceland is surprisingly full-bodied, with the aroma and dryness of both British and German hops (4.0% w; 5.0% v). Sadly, this beer is brewed only for the export market, although it does occasionally find its way into the bar at the local airport, and is available to NATO troops. Within Iceland, only near-beer may be marketed (maximum 1.8% w; 2.25% v), although travelers abroad are allowed to return with a dozen bottles of something stronger. Polar beer is produced by a locally owned brewery called Egill Skalla-grimsson, founded in 1913.

Polar Beer***

PRIPPS, *Bromma, Sweden.* The dominant brewing company in Sweden, with eight plants. Pripps has about twenty products spread over the three strength categories imposed by law. In the highest of these brackets, class III (maximum 4.5% w; 5.6% v), the company has a modestly hoppy product called Pripps Export, a more full-bodied Three Towns Export, a light, bland beer called Chess, and a malty, darkish product of indefinable style called Dart. In the second class (2.8% w; 3.5% v), the regular beers are augmented by the pleasant mild Carnegie Porter, of Scottish origin, and a rather disappointing Christmas beer, Julol. (Class I beers contain no more than 1.8% w; 2.25% v.) Pripps is partly owned by the state, and there are about a dozen smaller private breweries.

Pripps Export** Three Towns Export** Chess* Dart***
Carnegie Porter*** Julöl*½

RINGNES, *Oslo.* The best-known, internationally, of the Norwegian brewing companies. Ringnes is owned by the same group as Frydenlunds, of Oslo, which also produces Schou beer. The basic pilsener-type beers of all three are clean, dry, and sometimes have a flowery hoppiness.

Ringnes Pilsener**½

TUBORG, *Copenhagen, Denmark.* The other famous name in Danish brewing. While Carlsberg's beers are generally so round and mild as to be something of a style in themselves (albeit rather restrained), Tuborg's are crisper, drier and hoppier, thus having a greater fidelity to the classic pilsener type but arguably a lesser personality of their own. This is probably most evident in the Tuborg Gold produced in Copenhagen (4.6% w; 5.7% v). Tuborg has ten brands in the Danish market, a further five produced specifically for export, and about a dozen brewed overseas. The range is similar to that of Carlsberg, though that brewery's Elephant, for example, is matched by a slightly stronger product called Fine Festival, and known in some export markets as Royal Denmark (6.2% w; 7.75% v).

Tuborg's products have had a rather complicated marketing history in Britain, and in the U. S. are brewed by Heileman. Through Tuborg, United Breweries of Copenhagen is linked to the Rupert Group, which has international interests in drinks and tobacco, and is based in South Africa.

Tuborg Gold**½ Royal Denmark***

BELGIUM

The greatest variety of styles, the most gastronomically interesting specialties, and the most unusual beers in the world are produced in Belgium. Methods long forgotten elsewhere are still practised, and nowhere else have the idiosyncrasies of craftsman brewing survived so well.

If other nations has such attributes, they might proclaim them, but the Belgians have allowed the rest of the world to remain largely in ignorance. Some people in other countries are vaguely aware that the Belgians enjoy beer, but the renown of their products has not spread to any great extent beyond the culturally sympathetic north of France and The Netherlands. Only in recent years have imports from Belgium begun to establish any name at all in Britain and the U.S., and in neither country are they properly appreciated.

Visitors have been known to spend time in Belgium without experiencing the true joys of the country's beer, simply because they have been intimidated by the nation's cultural and linguistic introversion. In the northwest, the Flemish provinces, the language is basically Dutch; in the southeast, the region of Wallonia, French is spoken; on the German border, there are places where German is the local tongue.

In none of these regions is it enough to ask for a "beer" unless you want a very ordinary, though perfectly acceptable, pilsener. Although it sometimes seems that every cafe in the land advertises the Pilsener produced by Stella Artois, each also displays a beer menu. It is necessary to examine it and decide whether you want a refreshing wheat beer (a gueuze-lambic or perhaps a "white" from Hoegaarden), a special ale of one style or another (brown, pale, or saison; Belgian, "English," or "Scottish" in style), or a strong Trappist brew.

Even the least ambitious cafe is likely to offer five or six styles of beer, although perhaps only one brand of each. Some offer many more. There are about 100 brewing companies in Belgium, owning around 140 plants and producing several hundred brands. There have been a great many closures in recent years and some much-loved brews have passed to new owners, undergoing changes of character in the process. For that reason, judgment of some Belgian brews must be reserved for the moment. An example is Cristal Alken, Belgium's outstanding, pilsener-type beer, which has now been taken over by Kronenbourg.

Some brewers of the more specialized beers work only in the winter, and their products may, like wines, vary between good years and bad. Thus reputations change, and at a given moment the most interesting product in the land may be a prize vintage from a tiny brewery whose name is whispered by the cognoscenti in the specialty beer bars of Brussels or Antwerp. Meanwhile, there are a couple of dozen breweries that command a more permanent place in the drinker's attention, either by the consistent quality of their products or simply by their inescapable size within the market. (In the latter class are Artois, Jupiler, and Maes.)

ANTWERP AND FLANDERS

So distinctively different are the top-fermenting specialties of Flanders that each is almost a style in itself. This extraordinary variety dates back to the time when every town or village liked to boast of its own specialty. That phenomenon seems to have survived best in this part of the country. In the sense that they are mashed with barley in the conventional manner and are top-fermenting, all of these specialties might loosely be described as ales, but such is their individuality that in Belgium they are identified only by their own names.

DE KONINCK, *Antwerp.* The brewers of an outstandingly well-made, robust, top-fermenting beer that is first cousin of the Düsseldorf type of altbier and a more distant relation of English ale. Antwerp is the second city of Belgium and the Flemish capital, but it has only this one brewery, which restricts itself to one product. De Koninck's beer (4.16% w; 5.2% v) is a copper-coloured, all-malt brew, made with an infusion mash, with both the palate and aroma of Saaz hops. The brew is warm-fermented and cold-conditioned. It must be tasted on draught, in an un-pasteurized condition. At the Pilgrim, a cafe opposite the brewery in Boomgardstraat, drinkers may sometimes add a pinch of yeast to their beer. The bottled version of De Koninck, which can occasionally be found outside Belgium, is pasteurized.

De Koninck****

DUVEL, *Breendonk.* Producers of one of the world's greatest beers, although the brewery will have to be careful to maintain its standards with the growth in the product's popularity. Duvel (Devil) is sinfully deceptive. It is as pale as innocence, thanks to the use of pilsener malts kilned on the brewery's own premises, but it is not a lager beer; it is top-fermented. With its immense *mousse*, it seems at first as soft as a pillow, but it packs a punch (6.7% w; 8.2% v). In its palate, it has a hint of the pear brandy Poire Willem refined by its having been conditioned cold, then warm, then cold again. Duvel is an all-malt beer, with an infusion mash, hopped with Saaz and Styrians. In Belgium, it is unpasteurized unless it carries a red label. Early exports to the U.S. have been pasteurized, but with the intention that the process might eventually be avoided. The unpasteurized version has a slight sediment. The brewery also produces a beer for the Maredsous monastery.

Duvel***** Maredsous***

LIEFMANS, *Oudenaarde.* The world's finest brown ale is the Goudenband Speciaal Provisie (5.2% w; 6.5% v) produced by Madame Rose at the Liefmans brewery in Oudenaarde. This historically interesting town is famous for its production of brown ales, a tradition originally bestowed by the local water, and the Provisie is the noblest of them all. It has lost a little of the typical Flemish "sour" dryness since Madame Rose took over as brewmaster a decade ago, but has developed in its stead the finesse of a Montilla. Madame Rose employs an extraordinarily slow brewhouse procedure that stretches to almost two days. She uses six different malts and four species of hop, and ferments in open copper vessels. The Provisie is warm-conditioned for eight to ten months, followed by at least half a year racked in the bottle. Provisie is then blended into a six-week version to provide the local Oudenaarde Speciaal beer (4.2% w; 5.25% v). Based on Provisie, Madame Rose also makes a distinctive and sophisticated cherry Kriek (around 6.0% w; 7.5% v).

Provisie***** Oudenaarde Special*** Liefmans Kriek****
Also recommended of this type: Oud Zottegem, when it can be found.

MAES, *Waarloos.* The brewery, owned by Watney, of Britain, produces a pilsener-type beer called Maes, as well as an abbey-style beer for the monastery of Grimbergen.

Maes**½ Grimbergen**

RODENBACH, *Roeselare.* The brewery produces the definitive example of the wood-aged "sour" beer typical of West Flanders. Its fine burgundy colour derives from the use of Vienna malts. A very light hopping is employed, so that the bitterness is muted. The Rodenbach top-fermenting

NORTH SEA

THE NETHERLANDS

⊕ Westmalle
● Antwerp
● Bruges
Flanders *(red beers)* ● Ghent ■ Mechelen *(white beers)*
⊕ Westvleteren ■ Roeselare
(dark brown ales) Louvain Hasselt
BRUSSELS ● Hoegaarden
● Oudenaarde *(lambic beers)*
● Mons ● Namur *(top-fermented beers)*
● Liège

WEST GERMANY

FRANCE

⊕ Chimay ■ Rochefort

⊕ Orval

LUXEMBOURG

Ⓝ

⊕ Abbey breweries
■ Brewing towns
Brewing regions

yeast, a mixture of three strains that has been used for twenty-five years, no doubt confers some of the distinctive palate, but the most important part of the process is a maturation of nearly two years in unvarnished oak vats, each as high as the ceiling. It is during this period that a lactic fermentation starts. After aging, the beer is bottled "straight" as Rodenbach Grand Cru (4.2% w; 5.25% v). It is also blended with a younger version to create the regular Rodenbach (3.85% w; 4.8% v). Having sought out a beer with the characteristic of slight sourness, some Rodenbach drinkers then add a dash of grenadine as a sweetener, as if they were Burgundians making a *kir*.

Rodenbach***** Grand Cru*****
Also recommended of this type: Bios.

OERBIER, *Diksmuide*. Those brewers are traditionalists who revive what had seemed to be lost. Oerbier (6.75–7.5% w; 8.0–9.0% v) is a dark, top-fermenting beer in a style reminiscent of an English barley wine, produced by a couple of young revivalists who took over the much-loved Costenoble brewery after it had closed. Early samples were warm-conditioned for three months. The product is available in the world's best-stocked beer bar, Het Grote Ongenoegen, in Antwerp.

TRAPPISTS OF ST. SIXTUS, *Westvleteren*. One of the five monasteries in Belgium that still brew on the premises, with the additional claim that it has the country's strongest beer (and one of the world's most potent). Unlike the other four monasteries, it has such a small output that it can cater only to the thirsts of the brothers, but it has thoughtfully arranged for further supplies of its beers to be produced by the nearby commercial brewery of St. Bernardus in order to meet secular demand. It has been suggested that the abbey's own product is better than that of St. Bernard, but this is highly arguable. From whichever source, these top-fermenting, bottle-conditioned, dark-brown, strong beers, in the Trappist style, are very well-made, with their own distinctive, zesty character. The two breweries are among those that label their products with the gravity in Belgian degrees, which provides a very rough indication of alcohol by volume. The beers are also named in order of holiness: Pater at 6.0°, Prior, at 8.0°; and Abt, meaning Abbot, at a potent 12°. To complicate matters further, much the same designations are used by the other local brewery, Het Kapittel, which produces its own highly distinctive range of superb top-fermenting, bottle-conditioned beers. Although these breweries are in a hop-growing area, all of their beers are characterized more by their yeasty, estery fruitiness.

St. Sixtus/Bernardus Pater*** Prior*** Abt****
Also highly recommended: Het Kapittel (range).

TRAPPISTS OF WESTMALLE The most "different" of the Trappist beers is the Tripel (triple) available as three top-fermenting products brewed at Westmalle. So highly regarded is this beer that several other brewers now informally use the term Tripel as a designation of style for something similar. The defining characteristic of the Tripel (6.4% w; 8.0% v) is its pale colour, deriving from the use of pilsener malts. Its other notable characteristics are a "bigness" and a slight fruitiness, both deriving from the use of candy sugar in the copper and again as a priming. The palate is very complex, with some bitterness from a hop blend of English Fuggles and German Spalt and Tettnang, while the aromatic nose derives from Hallertau hops. The beer has a second fermentation of between one and three months before being primed and given a *dosage*, after which it is warm-conditioned in the bottle for three or four weeks. The brewery's dark-brown Dubbel (5.6% w; 7.0% v) is surprisingly dry and with a good malt character. A superbly delicate "single", known simply as Extra, is, sadly, reserved for the use of the brothers.

Tripel***** Dubbel***
Also recommended: Vieille Villers Tripel and Witkap Pater Tripel.

BRUSSELS

No other city in the world has beers as remarkable as those that are local in Brussels. A dozen tiny breweries in the Senne Valley, one of them in the city itself and none more that a fifteen-minute drive away, maintain the tradition of brewing spontaneously fermenting wheat beers with strange designations like gueuze and kriek, faro and framboise, all variations on a brew known as lambic. These beers present that same puzzling marriage of simplicity and sophistication found in the peasant paintings of Bruegel, and they were probably being consumed in his scenes of Flemish life.

The breweries of the Senne Valley have slats in the roof, or sometimes simply missing tiles, so that the magic micro-organisms of the district can enter and the consummation take place. For this purpose, the mash (of 30 percent wheat and 70 percent barley malt) is allowed to spend just one night in an open vessel in the gable of the roof. The brewer does not add yeast, but a spontaneous fermentation takes place during a storage period of between three and six months for a "young" beer, and two or even three summers for a mature one. The storage and fermentation take place in large wooden casks kept in dusty galleries; these breweries are never excessively cleaned in case a vital micro-organism is disturbed.

In a few cafes in the countryside around Brussels, lambic is served "straight" (unblended). When young, it is intensely dry and often cloudy (or "foxy"), rather like a rough farmhouse cider from the West of England. As it ages, it becomes clearer, a great deal more complex, and fruitier. A true lambic is always relatively dry, but a more sweet *(doux)* blend *(panache)* may be offered. Until the period between World Wars, the traditional tipple of Brussels was a version sweetened with sugar and known as faro. This was also sometimes diluted with water, in which case it was known as mars. Sugar is still sometimes served separately, with a muddler.

Gueuze-lambic is a blend of young and old in the cask. This blending process causes a new, second fermentation that produces a much fruitier palate. If this second fermentation is allowed to continue in the bottle, a Champagne sparkle is created; this most popular version is known simply as gueuze. If the second fermentation is induced by the addition of cherries or raspberries, the end product is known as kriek or framboise, respectively.

After three to nine months in the cask, kriek has a pronounced cherry character, with some almondy tones from the pits; framboise has a huge bouquet. These beers are also normally bottled and racked in the brewery for a further three to nine months while they become drier and stronger and gain in Champagne sparkle.

Framboise makes a wonderfully delicate aperitif, and kriek is a traditional summer drink in Brussels and the surrounding province of Brabant. Although they are usually served in the summer, these products can begin production only in the winter because of the temperature and conditions required for their spontaneous fermentation. The yeasts are wild, so no two brews are ever the same, and since production is seasonal, different breweries enjoy particular years of ascendancy.

Despite the use of raspberries and cherries, even the framboise and kriek beers are hopped. However, the hop is used in a most unusual way in the production of the lambic family of beers. While in all other beers hops are primarily used for the specific purpose of conferring bitterness, for these beers they are aged for several years in order that they will not do so. Yet the beers are massively hopped; the principal role of the hop is, as it was years ago, to be a preservative.

The spontaneously fermenting wheat beers of the lambic family are all brewed in the province of Brabant, to the west of Brussels, while the conventionally yeasted "white" beers of Belgium are also produced in Brabant but to the east of the city. This tradition survives only nominally in the city of Louvain but vigorously a little further east in the village of Hoegaarden.

Louvain, a handsome university city, remains an important brewing center, although its principal contribution to Belgian beer today is the conventional pilsener-style Stella Artois. Best known outside Belgium by its French name, the city is locally referred to in the Flemish spelling, Leuven. It is at the center of linguistic dispute in a part of Belgium where the language "frontier" takes many twists and turns. For the visitor, the safest option is to speak in English.

ARTOIS, *Louvain.* One of Europe's major brewing groups and by far the biggest in Belgium. Its ubiquitous pilsener-type beer, Stella Artois, seems in recent years to have shed some of its yeastiness and developed a greater hop character. The Stella Artois brewery has a premium Danish-style lager called Loburg. The group also produces pilsener-type beers originating from the Wielemans and Chevalier Marin breweries, a couple of Belgian-style ales called Ginder and Vieux Temps, a top-fermenting beer in the style of Duvel under the name Ketje, and an abbey-type range known as De Leffe, within which Radieuse is the most interesting product.

Stella** ½ Loburg** Wielemans, Chevalier Marin* ½
Ginder, Vieux Temps** ½ Ketje***
Abbaye De Leffe Radieuse***

DE KLUIS, *Hoegaarden.* The last haven of the Belgian white beer (witbier) in both the Hoegaarden and Louvain styles. The village of Hoegaarden once had thirty white-beer breweries, but the last of them closed in 1954, and the tradition was lost until 1966 when a local man with some knowledge of the technique decided to open a small brewery producing Hoegaards Wit. This has a much higher percentage of wheat (40 percent) than the Berlin "white" beer and, remarkably, the mash is 10 percent oats as well as 50 percent barley malt. It is hopped with English Goldings for bitterness and Saaz for bouquet, but the aroma is garnished with coriander and Curaçao. A very distinctive top-fermenting culture is used, in open tanks, and the beer is warm-conditioned for a month before being give a *dosage* in the bottle. When young, it is faintly sour and sometimes a little cloudy, but with maturity it becomes *demi-sec* and almost honeyish, and gains a shimmering, refractive quality called "double shine." While the Hoegaards Wit is moderately strong (just under 4.0% w; 5.0% v) the brewery also has a stronger Grand Cru version (6.0% w; 7.5% v). So successful are the products of this revivalist brewery that proprietor Pieter Celis has been emboldened to resuscitate the "white" beer of Louvain, which was traditionally identified by the name of the town's patron saint, St. Peter. His Peeterman is similar in style to the Hoegaards Wit, but without the maceration of botanicals. The brewery also has an abbey-style beer called Benedict. All of these products are available in Brussels at the specialist beer cafe Au Pere Faro, at 442 Chaussée d'Alsenberg.

Hoegaards Wit***** Grand Cru**** Peeterman**** Benedict***

TRADITIONAL LAMBIC BREWERS IN THE SENNE VALLEY

For dedication to an elusive craft, the following breweries all deserve a top rating of *****; since their products vary according to the good years and the bad, a greater discrimination would be illogical.

BOON, *Lembeek*. Revivalist beer merchant Frank Boon is maintaining the traditions of the old De Vit brewery, with products that are effusive with aromatic esters and less sour than many of their contemporaries. His purist insistence on Schaarbeek cherries makes for a truly authentic kriek, which is dry without being acidic. The brewery also produces a framboise.

CANTILLON, *Anderlecht, Brussels*. You can visit this "museum brewery" during the lambic-producing season, between the months of October and May (telephone: 5214928). It is a wonderfully traditional brewery, and its framboise is outstanding.

DE KEERSMAEKER, *Brussegem.* This brewery produces a rather light, ale-ish interpretation of the lambic style.

DE NEVE, *Schepdaal.* The unfiltered De Neve can manifest a fine rocky head and an almondy bitterness. In ordering this product, identify it by its retention of sediment, usually described by the French word *fond*. The brewery produces filtered beers under a variety of names, including the evocative Caves Bruegel, and supplies the famous Café Bécasse, just off Brussels' Grand Place, at Rue Tabora. This brewery is a traditionalist outpost of the large Vandenstock company, which is better known for mass-produced beers in the gueuze style and principally for a brand called Belle-Vue.

DE TROCH, *Wambeek.* The product is slightly darker and fuller than most lambics, and a littly gassy.

EYLENBOSCH, *Schepdaal.* Produces extremely dry lambics, with some of that over-aged woodiness typically found in Rioja wines. Many varieties, emanating from a proud and purist brewery. In Brussels, some of these characterful products can be found at the delightful Café Spinnekopke, at Place Jardin aux Fleurs (closed weekends).

GIRARDIN, *St. Ulriks Kapelle.* Brewers of big, fruity, rather citric, lambics with a lot of personality. Emphatically recommended.

LINDEMANS, *Vlezenbeek.* On its U.S. export label, Lindemans describes itself as a farmhouse brewery, and this claim is throroughly justified. It is in whitewashed farmhouse buildings dating back to 1870, with some Brabant brickwork a century older than that. Even the brewhouse has an agricultural look. Like most of the lambic breweries, Lindemans is a family firm, and it has combined a traditionalist approach to production with considerable marketing enterprise. "We don't know yet whether our success in the United States will depend on faddism," says René Lindemans, "but we are meanwhile well established in France. They understand our beer there, because they are used to drinking Champagne."

MORT SUBITE, *Kobbegem.* For brewery and beer, the name is French for "sudden death". "From beer to bier," joke those devotees who have survived. Despite the banter, Mort Subite is no more potent than other lambics. The name refers to an abbreviated version of a dice game that was traditionally played at a still-famous cafe in Brussels. When the dice-players got a phone message recalling them to their office, they settled their game by "sudden death." The Café Mort Subite, a 1920s building looking like a rather grand railway station bar, is at 7 rue Montagne-aux-Herbes Potagères, Brussels, and is well worth visiting for genuine local character. Mort Subite beer is among the more widely available lambics, but is still produced by traditional methods.

TIMMERMANS, *Itterbeek*. Produces several beers, available in all Stella Artois cafes in the Brussels area. They are well-made, by traditional methods. Ask for the unfiltered versions.

VANDERLINDEN, *Halle*. A local specialty called Duivel (Devil), blended from a lambic and conventional top-fermenting beer, is the proud product of this brewery. Not to be confused with Duvel (a corruption of the same Flemish word, see p. 55.

VANDERVELDEN, *Beersel*. If you have ever used pine kernels in cooking, you may recognize a similar palate in the dry, acidic, lambics produced by this small house in an historically interesting village. Try also the house lambics at the Oude Pruim and the Drie Fonteinen.

Smaller Lambic Houses

The essence of lambic production is in the fermentation and blending. Some houses buy their wort from larger neighbours. Just as a small wine-maker might use a neighbour's press, these brewers also employ someone else's copper. Boon is one example, but there are several smaller houses that do this, among them De Koninck Brothers (nothing to do with the Antwerp brewer of the same name), Drie Fonteinen, Hanssens, Moriau, and Wets.

THE SOUTH

The French-speaking provinces of Belgium, straddling the Ardennes, are of great gastronomic interest. They are perhaps better known outside Belgium for their ham, pâté, and game, but they also produce some noble beers, among which their regional specialties are the saisons originally brewed for springtime and summer but now available all year round. These are often served in corked, Burgundy-shaped liter bottles and taste better if shared by two people. If the bottles are to be stored, they should be racked horizontally and kept at about 14° C (55° F). Pour gently, to restrain not only the sediment but also the *mousse*. Saisons are top-fermenting beers of a rich, amber colour. Although there is no standard original gravity for the style, they often start quite high and are warm-conditioned to a soft fruitiness. The other great beers of the south are produced in the region's three Trappist monasteries. Two of these abbeys have beers that are world classics.

DU BOCQ, BRASSERIE CENTRALE, *Purnode and Marbaix*. Saison Régal, the most widely available example of the style, is produced in these two old breweries, both owned by the same family. It is not the most efflorescent of saisons, not the strongest (4.5% w; 6.5% v), but it is a subtle, handcrafted beer. It is produced with 96 percent malt, a blend of pale and crystal, in an infusion mash. A very vigorous fermentation takes place, and the character of the brewery's single-cell top yeast is evident in the aroma of the finished beer, after a month's cold maturation and two or three weeks of warm-conditioning. There is some alcohol in the nose, and the palate is predominantly fruity. This is surprising, considering its weighty hopping with Kentish species in the copper and Hallertau and Saaz in finishing. The fruitiness is also interesting in the light of the extremely thorough attenuation.

Among the range of bottle-conditioned beers produced by this company, one is of the "Scottish" type of Christmas ale that is popular in Belgium (6.8% w; 8.5% v). (Ironically, this type of strong ale is not available in its home country, although products brewed in Scotland exclusively for the Belgian market are well worth trying, especially Gordon's (about 7.2% w; 9.5% v) and McEwan's Christmas Ale (7.92% w; 9.9% v).)Du Bocq also has a vaguely "English" ale, unusually pale for the style and patriotically called Winston (6.0% w; 7.5% v). There is also an outstanding product in the range by the unusual name of Gauloise. This is not an especially smoky beer; the name derives from the legend that in ancient times the most brave of all the Gauls were the Belgians. Gauloise (6.8% w; 8.5% v) is a strong-tasting ale with a deep copper colour and a malty nose. A similar product called Bush Beer, from the Dubuisson brewery, has an even higher alcohol content (around 8.0% w; 10.0% v).

Saison Régal**** Regal Christmas***½ Winston***½ Gauloise****

DUPONT, *Tourpes*. Demonstrating outstanding skills in the craft of top-fermentation, this little brewery produces the wonderful Saison Dupont, with a big, sharp bouquet and almost peppery fruitiness, and an excellent abbey-style beer called Moinette.

Saison Dupont***** Abbaye de la Moinette****
Also highly recommended: Saisons de Pipaix (very sharp), Double Enghien (firm, "meaty," and extremely dry), Union, Voison (remarkable head retention), and 1900 Lefèbvre.

JUPILER, *near Liège*. The second-largest group in Belgium, and brewers of a well-balanced pilsener-type beer that bears its name. Jupiler recently acquired Lamot, which produces a somewhat blander pilsener-type beer.

Jupiler**½ Lamot**

TRAPPISTS OF CHIMAY. The classic abbey beers are produced in this inspirational abbey brewery. Chimay has set a style and standard of "Trappist" brewing that is followed, to varying degrees, in the production of abbey-style beers elsewhere, both within the order and outside. The grounds of the abbey are also the last resting place of one of the world's greatest brewers, the Belgian Jean de Clerck. In his tradition, Chimay remains an establishment where brewing is treated as an art, but an academic one.

Father Thèodore, the present brewmaster, produces three beers, each brewed from an all-malt infusion mash. Their character is influenced by several interesting factors: the brewery uses the local soft, acidic water without any additives; its single-cell yeast, isolated in 1949, has a pronounced personality; in addition to the earthiness of Hallertau hops, there is a distinctively geranial quality, although the precise blend of its hops remains a guarded secret; and fermentation takes place at notably warm temperatures. The beers, all top-fermenting and copper-coloured, are primed and given a *dosage*. The basic Chimay, with the red crown-cork (or sometimes in a "wine" bottle), has a hint of that blackcurrant character of a cabernet sauvignon, and is full-bodied (around 5.3% w; 6.6% v). The version with the white crown-cork is completely different. It is well-attenuated and dry (6.0% w; 7.5% v), with plenty of hop bitterness and similar to the beer produced at the nearby monastery of Orval. The Chimay "blue" (7.0% w; 8.75% v) is also full-bodied and fruity, with a spicy "zinfandel" aroma that is a work of art. As with all bottle-conditioned beers, and especially those with a full body, these products do develop slightly in strength as time passes. The Chimay "blue" is vintage-dated. It reaches its peak after two years, although it will retain its condition for five. Ideally, it should be stored at about 18° C (66° F) and on no account should it be refrigerated. It should be kept away from light and handled gently when being served, so that the yeast sediment does not impose itself on the highly distinctive palate of the beer.

Chimay Red***** Chimay White**** Chimay Blue*****

TRAPPISTS OF ORVAL. The monastery makes only the one beer, identified simply by its skittle-shaped bottle and the name Orval. It is dry-hopped, triple-fermented, distinctive among Trappist beers, and as potent an aperitif as the best Italian *amaro*. There is, as it happens, a legend— Princess Mathilde lost a golden ring in a lake in the valley, and said that if God ever returned it to her, she would thank him by building a monastery. When a trout rose from the lake with the ring in its mouth, the Princess was as good as her promise.

The original monastery was sacked in the French revolution, and a new one built during the late 1920s. Never did a brewery look more ecclesiastical, and the purity of even the beer is guaranteed (by the Brussels School of Brewing). Orval (4.56% w; 5.7% v) starts with an all-malt infusion mash, but candy sugar is added in the kettle. Kent Goldings are used for bitterness. After the first fermentation, the beer is held at 14° C (59° F) for six weeks, during which time there is a new phase of activity. The beer is primed and re-yeasted to start a third fermentation in the bottle. The beer reaches its peak after a year, and three years is the optimum period for storage. It should never be refrigerated, and is best served at from 10°–15° C (50°–60° F). It is also possible to buy Orval cheese at the abbey shop, with one of the brothers serving behind the counter.

Orval*****

TRAPPISTS OF ROCHEFORT. The fifth genuine Trappist monastery brewery, producing a range of beers similar in style to the basic Chimay.

Rochefort 6°***½ Rochefort 8°***½ Rochefort 10°***½
Also recommended: Abbaye de Bonne Espérance, Cuvée de l'Ermitage.

The Beers of Luxembourg

There are two Luxembourgs. One is a province of Belgium; the other, next door, is a Grand Duchy and an independent country. Like the Belgians, the people of the Grand Duchy of Luxembourg are enthusiastic gourmands, claiming with justification that their kitchens dispense French quality and German quantity; gastronomically, there is much to be said for being between such nations. In beer, however, the style of Luxembourg is German, and the country even has a purity law modeled on the *Reinheitsgebot*. The typical product range of a brewery in Luxembourg includes a pilsener-type beer; a slightly more potent brew, perhaps in the Dortmunder style; and a strong lager, sometimes seasonal.

The biggest company, Diekirch, has substantial exports. Its products include a fairly big, clean-tasting pilsener-type beer, hopped with Hallertau, and the fine Zätec Red, lagered for three months and unpasteurized (3.9% w; 4.8% v). Diekirch also has a stronger lager called Premium (4.9% w; 6.1% v), which is sometimes available in the U.S. as a malt liquor. There are only half a dozen breweries in all. The others are Brasserie Nationale (formed by the merger of Bofferding and Funck-Bricher), Mousel et Clausen (in which Artois of Belgium has a small stake), Henri Funck, Battin, and the excellent little Simon brewery.

THE
NETHERLANDS

Probably the most widely known beer in the world is Heineken, which comes from Holland, although many of those who buy and serve it seem unsure from which country it originates. More than by any other means, it was by entering the U.S. market immediately after the repeal of Prohibition, long before most other European brewers considered such a move, that Heineken made its name international. It has consolidated its position in the U.S. market by remaining a genuine import, although it now faces the paradoxical problem there of being too popular to be chic. In some other countries, notably Britain, a licensed version of Heineken is produced that is rather different from the original.

In Holland, Heineken enjoys no cachet; it is a mass-marketed brand, and is looked upon as such by the consumer. The same is true of Heineken's corporate stablemate Amstel, and of the Anglo-Dutch brand Skol. Those three are the giants of the Dutch brewing industry. There is one middle-sized company—Grolsch—and about ten much smaller firms. Most of the minnows are not in Holland in the strictest sense, since that name properly refers only to two northern provinces of the country known as The Netherlands. The country's beer-culture is in the south, in the provinces of Brabant and Limburg, close to the Belgian border.

By virtue of its enormous exports, its location on the edge of Germany, and the acceptance of beer as its everyday drink, The Netherlands considers itself to be very much a brewing nation, but the choice of products that it offers is small, and it has made no stylistic contribution. Most breweries have the same basic range of products: a Pilsener (about 4.0% w; 5.0% v); a sweet Oud Bruin (Old Brown) (2.0–3.0% w; 2.5–3.5% v); sometimes a stronger Dortmunder-style beer, usually identified simply as a Dort (5.0–6.0% w; 6.5–7.5% v); and seasonally a Bock, in Dutch usually spelled Bok (around 5.0% w; 6.0% v).

These styles are augmented by the occasional specialty product, the numbers and availability of which have increased in recent years with the growth of a more discriminating interest in beer. The giants, in the past very arrogant indeed, have followed the lead of their British counterparts by switching to policies more accommodating to the beer-buff, and a boutique brewery movement has started. These developments have been encouraged by the formation of consumer campaign called PINT.

ALFA, *Schinnen, Limburg*. The strongest lager beer in The Netherlands is Alfa's Super Dortmunder (6.0% w; 7.5% v), an all-malt brew, employing Czech hops and lagered for three months. The company's regular lager, Alfa (4.0% w; 5.0% v), is also an all-malt brew, lagered for two months.

Super Dortmunder*** ½ Alfa***

AMSTEL, *Amsterdam*. Named after the river that flows into Amsterdam, this internationally known brewing company has a waterside location a stone's throw from Heineken. The two were deadly local rivals until Heineken bought Amstel a few years ago.

Amstel's basic pilsener-type beer is slightly sweeter than Heineken's, and has a shorter lagering time. There is also a premium product called Amstel Gold (4.7% w; 5.8% v) and one of the more agreeable "light" beers (2.8% w; 3.5% v). In The Netherlands, Amstel additionally has an Oud Bruin, and a Bock (5.3% w; 6.6% v) that is slightly stronger than the Heineken counterpart. Amstel is exported from The Netherlands to the U.S., although in Canada it may go into production at the Henninger brewery. It is produced by associate breweries or licensees in several other countries.

Amstel Beer* Amstel Gold** Amstel Light** Oud Bruin* Bock***

ARCEN, *Arcen, Limburg*. A revivalist company that reopened a defunct brewery in 1981 and started to produce naturally conditioned top-fermenting beers there. Early products were a copper-coloured ale called Old Limburg (4.4% w; 5.5% v), a beer in the Trappist Double style labeled Magnus (5.2% w; 6.5% v), and a Triple (6.0% w; 7.5% v). Since there was at the time only one other top-fermenting ale in The Netherlands, from the Trappist abbey, all three of these welcome newcomers qualified immediately as highly distinctive products in the Dutch market. (Soon afterwards, another revivalist brewer used the Trappist abbey to produce a top-fermenting ale under the name of Sloth (6.8% w; 8.5% v) which in old Dutch means castle, not laziness.)

Oud Limburgs**** Magnus**** Arcen Tripel****

BAVARIA, *Lieshout, Brabant*. A supermarket-oriented company that nonetheless takes the trouble to malt its own barley, and claims to lager for two or three months. The resultant products are disappointing, and there is a curious lack of differentiation between the palates of the Pilsener and Dortmunder brands. Bavaria, the largest of the small breweries, also produces an Oud Bruin and a Bock.

Bavaria Pilsener**½ Dortmunder* Oud Bruin* Bock*

BRAND, *Wijlre, Limburg.* The oldest brewing company in The Netherlands, dating back to 1340 and producing some well-respected beers in a beautiful all-copper brewhouse. Its Pils, with a relatively small content of corn (11 percent) and lagered for six weeks, is notably light and clean, though only moderately hopped. An all-malt beer with the silly name Brand Up '52 (4.3% w; 5.4% v), also lagered for six weeks, has an excellent dry, hoppy palate. An all-malt beer called Imperator (5.0% w; 6.3% v), less of a doublebock than a Märzen, is lagered for eight weeks. It has an excellent maltiness, and is only lightly hopped. None of these beers is pasteurized.

Pils*** Brand Up '52***½ Imperator****

BUDEL, *Budel, Brabant.* An excellent little family brewery producing malty, unpasteurized beers. Even the Oud Bruin gets an eight week lagering. The Pilsener gets eight to ten weeks, and an excellent Bock (5.6% w; 7.0% v) gets twelve.

Oud Bruin** Pilsener*** Bock****

GROLSCH, *Groenlo, Gelderland.* That eyecatching, pot-stoppered bottle owes its survival not to gimmickry but to consumer conservatism. The brewery tried to phase out the pot stopper thirty years ago but was halted by resistance from its customers. "Being typical Dutch Calvinists, they didn't want to think they had to drink the whole bottle at once," jokes one of the directors of the family-owned company. Today, despite having to build some of its own equipment for the purpose, Grolsch gratefully persists with the pot stopper for its principal bottle size. The attention-catching value of the bottle is a mixed blessing, though, in that it distracts attention from the contents. Grolsch is a remarkably fresh-tasting beer, thanks to the brewery's adamant refusal to pasteurize, even for export. The beer's stability is ensured by ritualistic care in the brewhouse and fermentation procedures, and by a lagering time of between six weeks and two months. The lack of pasteurization helps highlight a firm Hallertau bitterness; although Grolsch has lost a little hop character in recent years, it remains drier than most Dutch beers. The house yeast imparts a characteristic underlying fruitiness. The brewery has an Oud Bruin and a malty Bok, but it is best known for its principal Pilsner product.

Grolsch Pilsner***½ Oud Bruin** Bok***

GULPEN, *Gulpen, Limburg.* An old-established small brewery making a range of good beers, all unpasteurized. Its most interesting products are a wonderfully bitter, hoppy, all-malt premium beer with a good nose, lagered for ten weeks, and with the silly name of X-pert (4.0% w; 5.0% v), and a Bokbier (5.5% w; 6.8% v) that can sometimes be found on draught. The bock, big and roasty with a well-retained head, is malty but also dry and is lagered for ten weeks. Gulpen also has a malty Dort (5.5% w; 6.5% v).

X-pert**** Bokbier**** Dort***

HEINEKEN, *Amsterdam.* In the Heineken family since 1864 and now with associate companies or licensees in twenty countries. This brewery's principal product in both Dutch and export markets is the pilsener-style Heineken beer (4.0% w; 5.0% v) that is dry without having a great deal of hop character. At its best, this Heineken seems to have some of the saltiness of the Czech original, but it also has its markedly fruity undertones. Although it has its own specific character, Heineken makes no special contribution to the pantheon of beers. The brewery also produces a rather thin-tasting Special Dark (4.0% w; 5.0% v), an Old Brown (2.0% w; 2.5% v), and several bock beers of around 4.8% w; 6.0% v. The brew called simply Heineken Bok seems to be the sweetest, Hooijberg a little drier, and Sleutel to have the best hop character, but as once-a-year brews, these are likely to vary from year to year. Heineken also produces a Stout called van Vollenhoven's (5.1% w; 6.4% v) that is made by the lager method but nonetheless makes a credible attempt at a top-fermenting palate. It isn't the greatest of stouts, but it makes a change.

Heineken**½ Special Dark* Oud Bruin* Heineken Bok**½
Hooijberg*** Sleutel*** van Vollenhoven's Stout***

HENGELO, *Hengelo.* One of two small breweries in The Netherlands owned by the Belgian group Artois. The other is Dommels. In the local market, Artois has a product called Special Dutch, a sweetish premium beer.

Hengelo Pils* Dommels Pils* Special Dutch*½

DE KROON, *Oirschot, Brabant.* A farmhouse brewery when it was founded in 1627, and still very small. De Kroon's Pils is agreeable but forgettable, and its premium Briljant bears more than a passing resemblance to Gulpen's malty Dort.

Pils*½ Briljant**½

DE LEEUW, *Valkenburg, Limburg.* A very well-respected producer of unpasteurized beers. A beer called Super Leeuw, (4.7% w; 5.9% v), well-rounded in the Dortmunder style but with a delicate bitterness, is especially well-liked. Super Leeuw is lagered for eight weeks. A full-bodied, typically sweet old brown called Donker gets seven to eight weeks, and a rather mild pilsener-type gets six.

Super Leeuw**** Donker (Old Brown)*** Pilsener**½

LINDEBOOM, *Neer, Limburg*. The name means Linden Tree. The brewery is noted for its dry pilsener-type beer, which has some of the bitterness of Tettnang hops as well as a pleasantly yeasty fruitiness. This and an excellent dry Bock (5.2% w; 6.5% v) are both lagered for ten weeks, and unpasteurized.

Lindeboom Pilsener***½

ORANJEBOOM, *Rotterdam*. One of two old-established and internationally known Dutch companies that now belong to the British group Allied Breweries, the other being Drie Hoefijzers, in Breda. Allied Breweries' principal label in The Netherlands is Skol, but some products are still produced under the old names. The brewery has a sweetish product called Oranjeboom-Royal (5.2% w; 6.5% v) in the local market, and two drier beers, Pilsner De Luxe (3.97% w; 4.9% v) and Special (4.7% w; 6.0% v) for export. It also has a bottom-fermenting product called Extra Stout (4.7% w; 6.0% v) that is broadly of the sweet type. The export products are all prefixed with the words Holland Beer. All the Oranjeboom beers are lagered for between three and six weeks, and are pasteurized.

Oranjeboom-Royal**½ Pilsner De Luxe*½ Special**
Extra Stout***

DE RIDDER, *Maastricht, Limburg*. This small brewery in the Hanseatic city of Maastricht, capital of Limburg, produces a creamy, fruity, Dortmunder-style beer (5.0% w; 6.25% v), lagered for three months and with the curious name of Maltezer, and a fresh-tasting, full-bodied Pils (3.7% w; 4.6% v) lagered for four weeks. Both their noteworthy products are unpasteurized.

Maltezer***½ Pils**½

SKOL, *Breda, Brabant*. The brewery is, with Oranjeboom, a part of Allied Breweries. Skol itself is bland and sticky, but the brewery also produces a very agreeable all-malt beer under the famous old name of Drie Hoefijzers (4.0% w; 5.0% v) that is dry and bitter and lagered for eight weeks.

Skol* Drie Hoefijzers***

TRAPPISTS OF SCHAAPSKOOI, *Tilburg, Brabant*. This abbey was founded in the 1890s, and has brewed ever since. During the 1970s, the brewery was operated in association with Artois of Belgium, but it is now back in the hands of the monks themselves. It produces a top-fermenting, bottle-conditioned Trappist ale (5.2% w; 6.5% v) with something of the yeasty character of the brews produced at Chimay, Belgium.

La Trappe****

BRITAIN & IRELAND

Most of the world drinks beer made by the lager method, which is Germanic in origin; Britain sticks to ale. This difference in custom is not always well understood, but it is a very clear distinction, and one that makes life more interesting, especially for the British.

When the rest of the world was switching to the "new" method a century ago, Britain was too powerful and proud to take foreign ideas seriously. Even today, and despite intense advertising, the style of beer favoured by the rest of the world has less than a third of the British market. It is true that internationally styled lager beers expanded their share considerably in the 1970s, but that growth has now slowed. The overwhelming preference of British drinkers is still for ales, which have around two-thirds of the market. There is also a small market for stouts, as a popular specialty item.

Like any other country, Britain takes for granted its own drinking habits, but they are often a surprise to visitors. Not only do the British prefer ales, they emphatically prefer to drink them on draught, in the pub. More than 75 percent of beer sold in Britain is served on draught, almost all of it consumed in pubs or working men's clubs.

In order to satisfy demand, a brewery of any size has to provide lagers, ales, and stouts, usually in several strengths and varieties, and even the most strenuous efforts of the marketing men have been unable to create any single brand that is the undisputed leader in overall beer sales. Attempts to achieve this, often backed by the greatest talents in advertising from both sides of the Atlantic, have met with humiliating failure.

This is all the more extraordinary when it is taken into account that half of all outlets are actually owned by the "Big Six" brewers. This situation, which is forbidden by law in the U.S., theoretically ensures that the big brewers can dictate, by means of availability, which beers the public should buy. In practice, they have been unable to do so. The omnipresence of the Big Six (Bass, Allied Breweries, Whitbread, Watney, Courage, Scottish & Newcastle) has irritated and alienated the consumer, and led to a favouring of the tiny indepen-

71

dents. Today, all of the giants have unused capacity, but some of the independents are unable to meet demand.

The giants themselves have more than forty breweries, some operating as subsidiaries with their own names, but there are also more than seventy old-established independents, owning about eighty breweries. There are also between fifty and sixty tiny boutique breweries, a great many of them established during the 1970s and 1980s. There are thus 170–180 operating breweries in total, with around 135 different owners.

The salvation of the independent brewers was a spontaneous consumer movement known as the Campaign for Real Ale (CAMRA), started more than a decade ago, and now passed its peak simply because its initial aims have been realized. (Perhaps the consumer should remember that the price of diversity and integrity is eternal vigilance.)

"Real" and Cask-Conditioned Ale

The term Real Ale is broadly understood by the British but confusing to the drinker from another country. It refers to an ale that has not been rendered stable by having been filtered, pasteurized, or chilled. The serious beer-drinker in Britain regards a stable ale as a dead ale, and prefers the ale to be alive and to mature in the cask or bottle. Most Real Ale is matured in the cask in the cellar of the pub. The term Real Ale is embarrassing to brewers, since many also produce the other kind. They are inclined to describe their Real draught ales as being cask-conditioned, and their filtered, chilled, pasteurized versions as being keg beers. These two similar terms, both referring to beers on tap, can again puzzle the uninitiated, but an understanding of them is essential to the proper appreciation of British ales. The majority of great British ales are on tap, but in cask-conditioned form, not as keg beer.

Traditionally, all brewers offered the drinker a choice of at least two distinctly different styles of basic draught ale. These were identified by the self-describing terms mild and bitter. In recent years, the popularity of mild has diminished, although it still maintains a hold in the Manchester area and the West Midlands (Birmingham, Wolverhampton). Mild is produced in two versions, the one pale (copper-coloured) and the other dark (opaque brown).

At least 80 percent of draught ale sold in Britain is bitter, and most breweries produce more than one version. The "ordinary bitter" may have as its bottled counterpart "light ale" (in Britain, this term has nothing to do with low-calorie beers). The "special" or "best" bitter may have as its counterpart a "pale ale" (again, a rather misleading adjective) or an "export". If there is an extra-strong bitter of some sort, it may be bottled as an "India Pale Ale", or under some fancier name. There may also be a full-bodied, strong, and often dark "winter" or old ale. This might have a bottled counterpart, often stronger still, known rather colourfully as a barley wine.

The drinker's choice is likely to depend upon the occasion or mood. The "ordinary bitter" will probably be favoured if a group of three or four friends meeting in the pub each intends to buy at least one round of drinks over a session lasting much of the evening. A stronger "special" or "best" might be considered if just one or two are to be consumed as an appetizer before dinner. An extra-strong specialty is especially acceptable as a winter-warmer or a nightcap. Although bottled ales are occasionally consumed in the pub, to add yet further variety, they are more commonly regarded as being something to take home.

The British ale-drinker is not only catholic in matters of style but also likes to sample the products of as many different breweries as possible. Since there are around 1,000 different beers available, more than 400 of them in the form of cask-conditioned draught ale, the drinker who enjoys traveling and exploring can have a great deal of pleasure. As an added dimension, the palate of a single cask-conditioned ale will vary slightly from one pub to another, and even within one barrel; a pint drawn soon after the barrel has been tapped will have a fresher and hoppier taste, and one drawn near the bottom of the cask may be maltier or more acidic. Some drinkers like their beer especially fresh, while others enjoy that maltiness at the end of the barrel, but a cask-conditioned ale that strikes an especially delicate balance is at the peak of its condition, and this is often commented upon in the pub. In the matter of cask- or bottle-conditioned ales, the pleasure of sampling would be diminished by the consistency beloved of U.S. brewers. A beer, after all, can be consistently boring.

LONDON AND THE SOUTH

The capital itself was once a great brewing city. Among today's national giants, several began either in London or in the nearby brewing town of Romford, as long as two or three hundred years ago. Trumans has been brewing in the same neighbourhood of the East End since 1683, though its associate Watneys, arrived on the scene as recently as 1836. Whitbread, no longer brewing in the capital but still very London-minded, began in 1742. Charrington, now subsumed into Bass of Burton, dates back to 1766. Ind Coope, also with a brewery in

Regional Differences

Each region of Britain has beers of a slightly different character than those of other regions. Although every brewery has products that occupy positions within a spectrum ranging from dry to sweet, the entire spectrum move several degrees to one side or the other, depending upon geographical region.

In most cases, both the character and the region are easy to define, but there are odd patches of Britain that cannot readily be labeled but that have ales especially worthy of attention. The most noteworthy region is Oxfordshire and the Cotswolds, a part of the country that is not decisively in either the South or West, but doesn't really belong to the Midlands, either. It is an area popular with visitors to Britain, and it has some fine breweries, like Morrell's of Oxford (known for their best bitter, under the name Varsity, and a strong winter brew called College Ale); Morland's of Abingdon (three excellent ales); Hook Norton of Banbury (very traditional, with a fine old ale); and Donnington of Stow-on-the-Wold (Britain's prettiest brewery, with characterfully crafted products).

The strength of a beer is not always evident in Britain, because it is not governed by law, and breweries are not obliged to reveal, or even to know, exactly how strong their beers are. It is unlikely that they don't know, but by no means impossible, since all they are required to declare (for tax purposes) is the original gravity, often referred to simply as the OG. In any event, the strength of a cask-conditioned beer will increase marginally as it continues, very slightly, to ferment (or "work") in the cellar of the pub. The original gravity gives a clue to the strength of a beer, though it is nothing more than a rule of thumb. The last two figures often give an indication of the alcohol content by volume. Thus, a low-strength ale, probably a mild, might have an OG of 1035 and an alcohol content by volume of 3.5 percent. An ordinary bitter is more likely to be nearer to 1040, with a strength approaching 4.0 percent by volume. A "special" or "best" might be around 1045 (4.5 percent), and extra-strong bitter 1050 (5.0 percent), a winter or old ale nearer to 1060 (6.0 percent), and a bottled barley wine anything from 1070 to 1100 (7.0–10.0 percent).

Burton, has its origins in 1779. Courage has just closed its London brewery, therefore casting doubt on the future of its magnificent Imperial Russian Stout*****(OG 1101.8)

The links between several London breweries and those in the faraway small town of Burton, in the Midlands, were forged in the 19th century. The London brewers, then known for their dark-brown beers, wanted also to offer the "pale ales" for which Burton was famous. These links were the beginnings of

Notable Brewing Centers

Brewing towns
Types of beers

national brewing groups in Britain, although the con-
solidation trend did not reach its peak until the 1960s.
Throughout it all, two small family breweries in London
have managed to retain their independence. They are
Young's and Fuller's, both beloved of ale-drinkers. In
recent years, several boutique breweries have started in
London, among them Godsons, Tower Bridge, and
Chudleigh.

Probably because London's backyard included the
hop-gardens of Kent, its beers, and those elsewhere in
the South and East, tend to be very dry. However, the
tradition of dark beers has long gone, and the most
famous London ales are conventionally pale bitters.

BRAKSPEAR, *Henley-on-Thames.* Produces English country ales
as fine as can be found anywhere, with that slightly
"rough" rural character, a well-attenuated hoppiness,
and an almost aggressive bouquet. The brewery has some
delightful little pubs in and around the famous regatta

town, and its products can be found in some specialist outlets in London. Brakspear's "ordinary" bitter, sometimes identified at Pale Ale (OG 1035), is a classic of its style.

Brakspear's Pale Ale*****

BRUCE'S, *London*. Supplies home-brew at three London pubs, though more are opening. From the bar at the *Fox and Firkin*, in Lewisham High Street, it is possible to see the brewery through a porthole. At the *Frog and Firkin*, in Tavistock Crescent, Westbourne Park, the tun and copper can be glimpsed through a hatch in the floor. These two breweries have a full mash, but the one at the *Goose and Firkin*, in Borough Road, uses malt extract. Bruce specializes in strong ales with colourful names like Dogbolter (1060), and brews a couple of Porters (1038). Though the beers lack complexity, the pubs are a must for the visitor to London.

Dogbolter*** Porter****

COURAGE, *London*. The London brewery has recently been closed, therefore casting doubt on the future of its magnificent Imperial Russian Stout (1101.8). The company's breweries in the West of England are still in production (see pp. 84–85).

Imperial Russian Stout*****

FULLER, *London*. Brews wonderfully complex and distinctive ales. Visitors to London may well pass the brewery on the road from the airport. The Extra Special Bitter (1055.75), known to drinkers simply as ESB, is the strongest regular pale draught ale in Britain. Its London Pride (1041.5) is a meaty "special bitter" often drunk as a session ale. Both combine a big hop character with an underlying sweetness. The "ordinary" Chiswick Bitter (1035.5) is lighter, with a leafy hoppiness.

ESB***** London Pride*** Chiswick Bitter***

GALE, *Portsmouth*. Home of idiosyncratic ales of high quality. The bottle-conditioned Prize Old Ale (1095), sweetish and almost herbal in its esteriness, is one of Britain's classics. This product is aged in wood for a year. The purchase of the Angel Steam brewery many years ago has recently inspired Gale's to use that name on a product for the U.S. market. Since this use of the term steam refers to power, and not to the style of the beer, this may cause some confusion. The company has a couple of excellent, distinctive bitters.

Gale's Prize Old Ale*****

IND COOPE, *Romford*. A national giant (part of Allied Breweries) that has recently revived three distinctly different ales from breweries that the company has acquired and closed over the years. These are Benskins, Friary Meux, and Taylor Walker, all fairly hoppy (all 1037).

Benskins*** Friary Meux*** Taylor Walker***

SHEPHERD NEAME, *Faversham, Kent.* Located in a hop-growing county, as the character of its ales suggests. It is doubtful whether there are any more hoppy ales in Britain than "Shep's" ordinary Bitter (1036) and "Best" (1039). They are so hoppy they are almost astringent and sharp, and provide perhaps the definitive example of this type of bitter.

Bitter****½ Best****

WATNEY, *London.* Because it seemed more eager than any other brewery to impose processed keg beer on the drinker, and to replace individuality with uniformity, Watney became the *bête rouge* of the Real Ale movement during the 1970s. Since then, the company has tried hard to throw off this mantle, but without total success. It might do better if, among its range of products, there were something a little more distinctive. Probably the company's best-liked product is its cask-conditioned London Bitter (1037.5) which, when well-handled, has a fine, hoppy nose. The higher-gravity Stag (1044) is less characterful. Another interesting product, under the Mann's label, is a brown ale that claims, with some justification, to retain more of the original character of this style than most of its contemporaries. Mann's has a gravity of 1034–35, as against the more common level of 1030–31. Although they are not especially interesting, Watney's two barley wines have something of a following: the pale Export Gold (1070) and the dark Stingo (1076).

Stag** London Bitter*** Mann's Brown***½ Export Gold** Stingo**½

WHITBREAD, *London.* Very much a London company, although it no longer brews in the capital. In Whitbread pubs in London and the South, ask for the products of the company's Fremlins and Wethereds subsidiaries, which are identified by name. Each of these breweries produces a good, hoppy, draught "ordinary" Bitter, although more promotional attention is apt to be given to Fremlins' big, smooth, dry "special" bitter called Tusker (1046) and to Wethered's distinctively pale and seasonal Winter Royal (1057). Elsewhere in the country, the sometimes vacillating Whitbread group has, in a number of cases, retained the individuality of the breweries that it has acquired over the years. Whitbread's nationally marketed products include two that are generally regarded as the definitive examples of their styles and might thus be deemed classics. These are Mackeson, the famous sweet stout (1042), and Gold Label (1098), a pale barley wine.

Fremlins' Bitter*** Tusker***½ Wethered Bitter*** Winter Royal**** Mackeson***** Gold Label*****

YOUNG, *London.* Revered by the Real Ale movement for its intransigent traditionalism during the worst years of the modernization mania. Such insouciance might be expected from an isolated rural brewery but Young's, with its steam engine, its working horses, and its pet ram for a mascot, is in the middle of London. The reward for its adherence to principle has been such a demand for its products that on occasion orders have to be refused.

Expansion to meet this demand might be one reason why its classically English "ordinary" Bitter seems recently to have lost some of its own unyielding character. Young's "ordinary" (1036) has traditionally had an almost flinty firmness and bitterness. Many drinkers prefer it to the maltier Special Bitter (1046), which is nonetheless an excellent beer. Young's also has a dark Winter Warmer (1055), which punches very hard for its weight when it is not slowed by diacetyl. The brewery also has an unusually good range of bottled beers. Young's should not be confused with the far larger Scottish firm of Younger's.

Young's Bitter***½ Special Bitter*** Winter Warmer****
Also strongly recommended: Harvey, McMullen, King and Barnes, Burt.

THE EAST

There is a remarkable collection of highly regarded breweries in the eastern bulge of the English countryside. Their products have recently become increasingly available elsewhere, but their original survival as independent and individualistic breweries is probably due to their being geographically out of the way. Like rare birds, they were protected by the terrain.

ADNAMS, *Southwold.* Said to produce the best beers in Britain by those who are given to making such simplistic statements. It makes a delightful outing to sample them on their home ground in the little harbor town of Southwold. Just to the south is Aldeburgh, home of the Britten-inspired June festival of music, and the larger town of Ipswich. Beer-writer Roger Protz has a great affection for the salty, tangy "seaweed" character he finds in Adnams' very hoppy but dexterously balanced Bitter (1036). A barley wine called Tally Ho (1075) is sometimes available on draught in the winter. Try also the bottled Broadside, a distinctively tawny strong ale.

Adnam's Bitter**** Tally Ho**** Broadside***

GREENE KING, *Biggleswade and Bury.* Every beer-buff in Britain knows the Greene family is that of Graham, not to mention his brother Hugh, the most liberal Director-General the BBC ever had and chairman of the brewery's board. The brewery is especially loved for its Abbot ale (1048), strong, very full-bodied but still hoppy, and possibly the most highly regarded individual product from any brewery in Britain. A subsidiary called Rayment's, in Hertfordshire, makes an unusual, tawny, malty ale called BBA (1036), which has its own devoted following.

Greene King Abbot**** Rayment's BBA***

RUDDLE'S OF RUTLAND, *Oakham*. The alliteration must have helped, not to mention the fact that Rutland is a country that audaciously survives in spirit after being eliminated from the map by the bureaucrats. It also happens that Ruddle's ales, the first British beers to achieve popular cult status, are the archetypal example of the country brewing style. Many drinkers prefer the "ordinary" Bitter (1032), with its gutsy hoppiness, to the strong, malty "special" (1050), which has the brand-name County.

Ruddle's Bitter ***½ County***
Also strongly recommended: Bateman, Elgood, Paine, Ridley, Tolly.

THE NORTH

There are three distinct styles in this region. *Yorkshire* beers tend to be very full-flavored and either creamy or round, sometimes as a result of the county's own regional system of fermentation in blue-slate "squares". Further north, though still within England, is the distinctive style of brown ale exemplified by that of *Newcastle*, while a cross-border influence manifests itself in the "Scotch" ales of the region. In the North-West, the very dry, hoppy ales of Manchester merit detailed exploration.

BODDINGTONS, *Manchester*. Famous for one of Britain's outstanding bitters. This revered product has a distinctively pale colour, and is superbly hopped to produce a dryness rather than a bitterness (1035). Hard to find outside its area, because the brewery is too quality conscious to take risks with the brew's unwillingness to travel.

Boddingtons Bitter****½
Also strongly recommended in the Manchester area: Holt, Hydes, Lees, Polland, Robinson.

CAMERON, *Hartlepool*. A serious-minded brewery producing a couple of excellent ales. Some drinkers prefer the delicately balanced Best Bitter (1036), with its slight hop emphasis, to the maltier Strongarm (1042). Cameron is in the same group as Tolly, in East Anglia.

Cameron Best Bitter*** Strongarm***

GREENALL WHITLEY, *Warrington*. The biggest regional brewer in Britain, based in an important brewing (and distilling) town near Liverpool. Its basic Local Bitter is described with some accuracy by the *Good Beer Guide* as being pleasant but undistinguished. A product of this brewery, marketed in the U.S. as Cheshire English Pub Beer, has little to do with the resonances of its name. In Warrington, Greenall has as its competitors the well-regarded independent Burtonwood Brewery and Allied's Tetley Walker subsidiary. Elsewhere in the country, Greenall owns the Shrewsbury and Wem Brewery, and Shipstone, of Nottingham.

Local Bitter*½ Cheshire English Pub Beer*½

Strongly recommended in the Liverpool area: Higsons.

HARTLEY'S, *Ulverston.* The Lake District and Cumbrian Mountains are on its doorstep, but devotees of this rustic brewery find it hard to leave the pub. Its "special" bitter, branded as XB, is a marvel of balance (1040). Malty, yes, but full-flavoured and complex. One of the lesser-known among the great ales of England.

Hartley's XB****

Also strongly recommended in Cumbria: Jennings. And, nearby in Lancaster: Mitchells, Yates & Jackson.

NEWCASTLE BREWERIES. Its Brown Ale (1045.1) made this brewery famous, although it is not so much brown as a Viennese amber. While other English brown ales are dark, opaque, very sweet, and low in alcohol content, this one is translucent and less sweet. This local specialty, in its distinctive clear-glass pint bottle, has been brewed since 1927. The origins of the style are not clear. Newcastle Brown's most obvious rival within the style, a product called Double Maxim brewed by the Vaux company of nearby Sunderland, was not introduced until 1938. There was, however, a beer simply called Maxim in the first decade of this century. Although Newcastle and Sunderland are in England, their beer styles have long been affected by cross-border influence from Scotland. Newcastle Breweries itself merged in the 1950s with the Scottish firms of McEwan's and Younger's.

Newcastle Brown Ale***

SAMUEL SMITH, *Tadcaster.* The classic "Yorkshire Stone Square" brewery. Fermentation takes place in a system of enclosed blue-slate square vessels, with a recirculation of the barm ale. This characteristic Yorkshire method produces rounded beers with a very full flavour and a clean, creamy head. The new appreciation of Real Ales in the 1970s raised "Sam's" sights from the level of a barely known rural brewery to the point where it is now exporting to the U.S. Pride in its achievement must be tempered with concern about such a rate of expansion. The principal product is the draught Old Brewery Bitter (1040), and there is a similar but stronger bottled version identified as a Pale Ale (1050). The Old Brewery Strong Brown Ale (1050) is in the Northeastern style (see also Newcastle above and Vaux, p.82). A Porter (1050) is being produced for the U.S. market, and the brewery also has a very strong golden-coloured beer in the barley-wine style, called Strong Golden (1101).

"Sam's" should not be confused with its neighbour John Smith's. The two were once rival branches of the same family, but "John's" is now part of the Courage group, and its products are, sadly, no longer of great interest. There is a third brewery, belonging to Bass, in Tadcaster, which is itself little more than a village. Tadcaster is close to York, one of England's most attractive and historically interesting cities, and a base from which to explore the Yorkshire Dales.

Old Brewery Bitter**** Pale Ale***½ Strong Brown**** Porter***½ Strong Golden***½

TETLEY, *Leeds*. Another "Yorkshire Square" brewery, accorded by beer-lovers a degree of affection rarely given to member-companies of national groups (in this case, Allied Breweries). The same is true to some extent of nearby Webster (a Watney affiliate), although it produces a smaller proportion of cask-conditioned ale. Tetley's soft Bitter (1035.5), with its light palate and tawny-pale colour, is typical Yorkshire ale. Tetley also has the Walker brewery in Warrington.

Tetley's Bitter***½
Also recommended in Yorkshire: West Riding.

THEAKSTON, *Masham, near Ripon, and Carlisle*. Famous for its Old Peculier, spelled with the penultimate "e". A classic example of old ale as a style, this brew has a wonderful profundity when tasted on draught in its native North Yorkshire, but doesn't travel well. So popular did Old Peculier (1058.5) become during the 1970s that Theakston's had to evict its Best Bitter, which it moved to the formerly State-owned brewery at Carlisle. Best Bitter (1038) still has a Yorkshire taste, despite its new Cumbrian home.

Old Peculier****½ Best Bitter***

TIMOTHY TAYLOR, *Keighley*. A craft brewery down to the last detail. Very small, producing a wide range of all-malt beers on the edge of the moorland Brontë country. All the draught is cask-conditioned, and the bottled ale is unpasteurized. The brewery's outstanding product is probably its "special" bitter, under the name Landlord (1043), though its Best (1037.5) is very popular. Golden Mild (1034) is also recommended. Taylor's has a notable winter old ale called Ram Tam (1043) and a Porter, at the same gravity, that is possibly the most successful of the revived porters.

Landlord****½ Best*** Golden Mild*** Ram Tam*** Porter****
Also strongly recommended in Brontë country: Goose Eye.

THWAITES, *Blackburn.* The mild ales produced by Thwaites have frequently been voted the best in Britain. This style remains popular in the North-West, and Thwaites upholds it splendidly, with Real Best Mild (1033) and Real Draught Mild (1031). The brewery also has an excellent bitter at 1035. Among its bottled beers, a brown ale called Danny Brown and an "old" ale named Old Dan are also well-liked.

Real Best Mild**** Real Draught Mild*** Bitter***
Danny Brown*** Old Dan***

VAUX, *Sunderland.* An ambitious regional company that owns breweries in the U.S. (Fred Koch of Dunkirk, NY) and Belgium (Liefmans) as well as in Scotland (Lorimers) and England (Ward and Darley, both in South Yorkshire). In its home country, it is notable for its North-Eastern style strong brown ale, Double Maxim (1044.4), and its Sunderland Draught Bitter (1040).

Double Maxim****   Sunderland Draught Bitter***

BURTON AND THE MIDLANDS

In the international world of brewing, the name of Burton upon Trent in renowned for the gypsum-rich water that made the town's pale ales famous. But even in Britain, the man in the street might have some difficulty in saying exactly where Burton is. It is a small and rather scruffy town that, for the fortunes of its brewers, has the good luck to be right at the heart of England, between heavily populated cities like Birmingham, Derby, Nottingham, and Leicester. Thus, this small Midlands town is the brewing center of England. The Trent Valley was known for its beers by the early 18th century, according to Defoe, and its pale ales were nationally famous a century later. The River Trent's principal city, Nottingham, still has three respected local breweries (Hardys and Hansons, Home, and Shipstone), which make it a pleasant place for the beer-drinker to visit. A much sweeter type of ale is characteristic of the West Midlands, around Birmingham, Wolverhampton, and Dudley, and these places are also well known for their milds.

BANKS, *Wolverhampton.* The Mild ale produced by this brewery has a nationwide reputation among beer buffs, although its tawny colour makes it hard to place between the normal classifications of dark and pale. A classic example of the region's tradition of mild ales, it is remarkably potent for a beer of 1036, and has a smooth, malty palate. The sweetness of Midlands ales often extends even to bitters, but Banks Bitter (1038.5) is relatively well-hopped.

Mild**** Bitter**½
Also strongly recommended: Batham, Holden.

BASS, *Burton.* Brewers of a world classic when it was the definitive Burton Union ale, but Draught Bass must now forfeit that status. The world's most famous pale ale brewery announced in 1981 that it would stop using the Burton Union System of fermentation because the maintenance costs were too high. Unions is the name given to the interconnecting oak casks in which the aristocratic Bass yeast exercised itself through a circulatory fermentation. This system is unique to Burton and is still used by the Marston's brewery there; perhaps they will continue to recognize the value in such a distinction.

In the Burton Unions, ale gains a distinctive finesse, and it is difficult to believe Bass will be able to replicate it by other means. Draught Bass (1044) and the bottle-conditioned India Pale Ale under the Worthington White Shield Label (1052) may remain good beers, but they will lack the distinction of having been produced by the Burton method. Whether the change will be perceptible in the export versions of kegged and bottled Bass is of less significance, since the enigmatic combination of freshness and maturity of the Burton Union products never did survive pasteurization. Neither factor is quite such a consideration in a product as robust as Bass's excellent barley wine (1092.4), though it is to be hoped that the company continues to give serious attention to the character of this product.

On the basis of the production of its several breweries in England, Scotland, Ireland, and Wales, Bass is Britain's biggest brewer (this calculation assumes, reasonably, the inclusion of Carling Black Label, a Bass brand in England).
Draught Bass**** Worthington White Shield****½
Bass No. 1 Barley Wine****

MARSTON'S, *Burton.* Unique in that it is the sole practitioner of Burton Union brewing (see Bass, above). No less than three British classics feature in its range: Pedigree, at (1043), is probably the most sophisticated special bitter in Britain; Merrie Monk (1043) is an unusually strong dark mild ale; and Owd Roger (1080), which had its origins in faraway Buckinghamshire at the *Royal Standard of England* pub in Forty Green near Beaconsfield, when that was a home-brew house. The beer, which is still served there, is the outstanding example of a draught old ale.
Pedigree***** Merrie Monk**** Owd Roger*****
Also recommended in Burton: Everards.

MITCHELL AND BUTLERS, *Walsall.* The only brewery in the world exclusively devoted to the production of mild ale. For that alone, its Highgate Mild (1034) must count as a world classic. It is also a fine example of the style, although tastings of mild ales fail to produce agreement as to which of five or six consistent favourites is the definitive example of this threatened style.

Three Notable Pub-Breweries

The visitor to this part of England should in no circumstances miss three pubs that have brewed their own ale for as long as anyone can remember. Each is interesting in its own right. The splendidly run *Old Swan*, with a superb beer, is near Dudley at Halesowen Road, Netherton. The *All Nations* pub is at Madeley, Telford, Shropshire. The *Three Tuns*, looking rather like a Baptist chapel, is in the Welsh border town of Bishop's Castle.

Mitchell and Butlers also produces a couple of bitters that are worthy of attention as examples of West Midlands sweet beers, though neither is outstanding: the stupidly named Brew XI (1038.8), produced at the company's Birmingham brewery, and the more complex Springfield Bitter (1035.9), from Wolverhampton. Mitchell and Butlers has retained the individuality of its products, despite being part of the Bass group.

Highgate Mild***** Brew XI*** Springfield ***½

PENRHOS, *Kington, Herefordshire.* Monty Python's favourite brewery. The earnings of Python performer Terry Jones helped finance this revivalist brewery, which is notable for its Porter (1050).

Penrhos Porter***½

THE WEST COUNTRY

The most touristic part of England is also the region that best demonstrates the beauty of boutique brewing, especially in the area of Bristol and Bath. Perhaps that is because cask-conditioned ales became hard to find there during the period when Courage was being heavy-handed with its monopoly in the mid-1970s. Highly regarded boutique brewers in the West include Archer, Butcombe, Golden Hill, Mendip, Nailsea, and Smiles. There is even a restaurant that brews its own beer: the *Miner's Arms*, at Priddy Wells, in Somerset. Further west, the *Blue Anchor*, at Helston, Cornwall, is the most historically interesting of all the home-brew houses.

COURAGE, *Bristol and Plymouth.* A national giant, but with its greatest strength in the South-West. The nationally available but Bristol-brewed Director's Bitter is one of Britain's leading cask-conditioned ales (1046), superbly balanced if with a very slight inclination to maltiness. The house esteriness is more evident in the Bristol-brewed Best Bitter (1039). The Plymouth brewery produces a very highly regarded mild called Heavy (1032). Plymouth is an unlikely location for a mild, and it's a pity this fine brew is not more widely available. Courage's outstanding, warm-conditioned, and rather citric Bulldog Pale Ale (1068) is produced in the company's biggest brewery, near Reading.

Courage Directors'***½ Best Bitter**½ Plymouth Heavy**** Bulldog****

ELDRIDGE POPE, *Dorchester.* Thomas Hardy's "Casterbridge" was actually Dorchester, and he even wrote about the local beer, lyrically and at length. For a Thomas Hardy festival in the 1960s, the local brewery produced a special bottle-conditioned old ale, and has done so at intervals ever since. Thomas Hardy's Ale is produced in a limited edition of numbered bottles as a laying-down beer. At a gravity of 1126, it is Britain's strongest beer (10% w; 12% v). The brewery also produces a strong draught called Royal Oak (1048), a hoppy draught called IPA (1041), and a Bitter (1032.5).

Thomas Hardy's Ale***** Royal Oak***½ IPA**½ Bitter**

WADWORTH, *Devizes.* A traditionalist brewery right down to the wooden casks in which 80 percent of the 6X, the company's best-selling, full-bodied ale (1041), is sold. Wadworth's Old Timer, at 1053, is also very popular, but there is much to be said for the hoppiness of the lower-gravity draught IPA (1035) and Devizes Pale Ale (1031). Wadworth's is the English country brewery at its magnificent best.

6X***½ Old Timer***½ IPA**** Devizes Pale Ale***
Also recommended in the West: Devenish, Gibbs Mew, Hall and Woodhouse, Palmer, St. Austell.

WALES

Two favourite breweries among British ale devotees are in Wales: Brain and Felinfoel. Another three also merit attention: Border, Buckley, and Crown. Despite the success of these five in tickling the palates of drinkers, Wales does not have its own distinctive style of ale, nor any brewery that distinguishes itself for a special contribution to the art. The designation Welsh Ale referred, in Anglo-Saxon times, to a beer sweetened with honey, but this practice is no longer widely reported in the Principality.

BORDER, *Wrexham.* Noted for its several mild ales. The one known simply as Border Mild (1032.4) has an agreeably

nutty palate. The brewery has a lightly hopped Bitter at
1035.4.

Border Mild*** Bitter **½

BRAIN, *Cardiff.* In a reader survey carried out by *What's
Brewing,* the newspaper of the Campaign for Real Ale,
Brain's SA (1040.6), a big, smooth, special bitter, was
widely nominated for attention. It is an ale with an
adventurous blend of drinkability and power. The brewery has a pleasant ordinary Bitter at 1035.5, and an
interesting dark mild called Red Dragon Dark (1035).

SA***½ Bitter*** Red Dragon Dark***

FELINFOEL, *Llanelli.* Double Dragon, a deceptively drinkable,
smooth special bitter is highly regarded. The brewery also
has a hoppy ordinary Bitter (1035) and a Mild (1032).

Double Dragon***½ Bitter**½ Mild**

SCOTLAND

Europe regarded Scotland as a great brewing nation
until its long-established traditions were battered by
mergers during the 1950s and 1960s. The modernizers
failed in their objectives, but did a lot of damage on the
way. Scotland still has its own stylistic identity, but only
a few wonderful beers remain. Scottish ales are characteristically fuller-bodied than those in England, empha-
sising the malt rather than the hop. While English ales
are generally a translucent copper colour, even the
palest among the Scottish ones are inclined to a tawny
profundity. While English draught ales are either "mild"
or "bitter", those of Scotland are "light" (in weight; often
quite the opposite in colour) or "heavy". These designations are further confused by a parallel system in which
ales are designated by the price, in shillings, that a cask
commanded in some long-gone happy day. Sad to say,
the strong Scotch ales produced for the Belgian market
are not available in their native land, although the style
is echoed in Fowler's Wee Heavy and Traquair House.

BELHAVEN, *Dunbar.* "The Burgundy of Scotland. Bavaria cannot produce the like", said the geographically eclectic
Emperor of Austria. It is true, though, that Belhaven is the
Chateau Latour of Scottish breweries, and it is to be
hoped that this will not be changed by the company's
recent move from the control of one corporate entrepreneur to another. Belhaven's rich 80/- (eighty shilling) is
the definitively Scottish draught ale (1042), although as a
masterpiece of brewing the more English-tasting 70/- is a
thing of beauty and astonishing balance (1036). There is
also an excellent 60/- (1031). The brewery sometimes

produces a draught version of its superb Strong Ale (1070). Belhaven ale occasionally finds its way to the U.S., where it is often made undrinkable by excessive chilling. This company's products are too complex and sensitive to survive that kind of treatment.

60/-***½ 70/-**** 80/-***** Strong Ale****½

DRYBROUGH, *Edinburgh.* Pentland 70/- (1036), named after the hills that guard Edinburgh, was introduced in 1981 in response to demand for a traditional cask-conditioned ale. Previously, the company, the Scottish arm of Watney, had produced only pasteurized beers.

Pentland***

LORIMER, *Edinburgh.* With its coal-fired copper and open-square fermenters, this delightful brewery produces an excellent 1076 strong ale for the Scottish and U.S. markets. The product is described as Golden Strong in its home country and as Traditional Scotch in the U.S. A big, malty beer, it survives U.S. chilling more than some, but it should be served at 11° C (55° F).Lorimer also produces an 80/- ale (1043) and a 70/- "Best Scotch" (1036.5). Lorimer ales are also available in the North-East of England, and the company is owned by Vaux, of Sunderland.

Golden/Traditional Scotch**** 80/-***½ 70/-***

MACLAY, *Alloa.* One of the two cherished independents of the Scottish brewing industry (the other is Belhaven). Like Edinburgh, Alloa is an historically important brewing town. Maclay's products are superb but often hard to find, and the brewery has always been concerned that they are not spoiled by excessive travel or careless handling. The regular draught beers are a Light (1030), a Heavy (1035), and an Export (1040), and there is an outstanding Old Alloa ale of 1065.

60/-Light**** 70/-Heavy**** 80/-Export**** Old Alloa****

McEWAN'S/YOUNGER'S, *Edinburgh.* Sister companies within the Scottish and Newcastle group. This is one of the Big Six British brewing groups, although it is far stronger in Scotland and the North-East of England than it is elsewhere. Its once great reputation has been blunted by the demands of mass marketing, but in recent years the group has made some gestures toward tradition. Its brands in the Scottish, English, and international markets are many and confusing, and the name McEwan is even spelled in two different ways. The company's products are nonetheless very Scottish in style. The cask-conditioned McEwan's 80/- Best Scotch (1043.5), in England known as Special, is agreeable, as are Younger's IPA (1043.5) and Younger's No. 3 (1042).

McEwan's Best Scotch*** Younger's IPA** No. 3**

TENNENT, *Edinburgh/Glasgow*. Lager has traditionally been more popular in Scotland than in England, and Tennent's seem to have been the pioneers of the style there, since they were producing this type of beer at their Glasgow brewery as early as 1888. The relatively full-bodied Tennent's Lager (1035.5–1037.5) is still probably the archetypal Scottish example. The company is now part of the Bass group; through mergers, Tennent's also inherited a much-loved strong ale called Fowler's Wee Heavy, originally brewed at Prestonpans but in recent years produced at several locations.

Tennent's Lager** Fowler's****½

TRAQUAIR HOUSE, *Innerleithen*. The brewery is in a castle in which Bonnie Prince Charlie once took refuge. Like any other large residence, it had its own brewery, and this amenity, which is at least 250 years old, was put back into use by the present Laird in 1965. The castle can be visited (telephone Innerleithen 830323), and its fine ale (1075–80) is found in the free trade. It is occasionally available bottle-conditioned or in the cask, and in either form is a classic example of a Scotch ale.

Traquair House Ale*****

IRELAND

The land of dry stout, as typified not only by the famous black brews from Guinness, of Dublin, but also by the similar products of its tiny rivals Murphy and Beamish, both in Cork, the republic's second city. The occasional dry stout can be found elsewhere in the world, but in no other country is it the principal style of beer. True enough, stout-brewing is also a tradition across the water in Britain, but there is a difference. English stouts are sweet, and represent a small specialty; Irish stouts are dry, and the country's everyday beer. More than half of all beer consumed in Ireland is dry stout, the rest being divided between the country's characteristically reddish-coloured ales (themselves a minor regional type) and conventional lagers.

Contrary to superficial impressions, stout is not simply a dark beer. With its roasted barley palate and its intense hoppiness, it is a distinct and major beer style. A dry stout is to the world of beer what a true amontillado sherry is to wine. Such a beer even deserves the same adjectives used by Hugh Johnson to describe a genuine amontillado in his *World Atlas of Wine*: "Dry and almost stingingly powerful of flavour, with a dark, fat, rich tang". Irish ales, by contrast, are markedly sweet. Although their existence as a minor type adds colour to the world of beer, they are not especially interesting and, since they are all pasteurized, they lack the character of their British counterparts. The stouts of Ireland usually have a gravity of around 1039; the ales, about 1036.

BEAMISH, *Cork.* The softest and lightest-tasting of the Irish stouts, with a very white head. The full name of the brewery is Beamish and Crawford, and it is owned by Carling O'Keefe, of Canada. The only Beamish brand is Beamish Stout, although other types of beer are produced under license from breweries elsewhere in the world.

Beamish Stout**** ½

GUINNESS, *Dublin.* The only Guinness brands are dry stouts, though there are several of them. As one of the world's largest brewers, Guinness is unique in devoting itself exclusively to such a distinctive product. Other styles of beer are not produced by Guinness except at arm's length through subsidiary companies or partnerships with other brewers. The defining characteristic of all Guinness stouts is an intense hoppiness that has somehow been married to the roasted-barley palate typical of the style. The unmistakable complexity of a good Guinness is the product of methods, including a remarkably slow brewhouse procedure, that were arrived at empirically over a couple of hundred years. The first Arthur Guinness was a brewer in County Kildare before moving to Dublin in 1759. The brewery that grew on the Dublin site is now the biggest in Europe, and it has made Guinness the world's largest exporter of beer. The Dublin brewery serves Ireland and all export markets, including the north of England, north Wales, and Scotland. The south of England and south Wales are served from a large Guinness brewery in London, and there are several plants and licensees elsewhere in the world.

It is often argued that the Draught Guinness (3.25–3.50% w; 4.0–4.5% v) produced in Ireland tastes better than that brewed in England. This is true but, contrary to rumour, it has nothing to do with holy water. Because of fast turnover, the company does not consider it necessary to pasteurize the beer in Ireland; hence its fresh character. In Britain, from whichever source, it is pasteurized. On both sides of the water, the creaminess in Guinness is aroused by a unique method of pressure tap, so in neither country is it "naturally" conditioned. For that reason, some devotees prefer the drier Anglo-Irish bottled version, subtitled Extra Stout (3.25–3.50% w; 4.0–4.5% v). What is lacks in creaminess, this bottle-conditioned brew more than makes up in finesse. An Irish Draught Stout (3.25–3.50% w; 4.0–4.5% v) and an Extra Stout, both pasteurized, (4.5% w; 5.5% v) are exported to North America.

Like any other company, Guinness does occasionally experiment with new products. Admirers of the company's products may be pleased that a Guinness "light"

89

briefly marketed in Ireland has now been withdrawn, but will be sorry that the product called Triple X and made available in Britain failed to find a sale. Triple X was essentially the same as the magnificent brew quaintly known within the company as Foreign Extra Stout (6.5% w; 8.0% v), the tropical version produced in Dublin for export and in breweries in the Caribbean, West Africa, and Asia. It is brewed from a very high gravity and then blended with stout aged in wooden casks so that its weight is mitigated by a hint of sharp, quenching sourness. The beer is then stabilized by pasteurization. There are several other minor variations on the theme of Guinness Stout, and the company has a controlling interest, with British brewery partners, in Harp Lager and a number of Irish ale brands.

Draught Guinness (Ireland)****½
Draught Guinness (Britain)****
Extra Stout (Britain and Ireland)*****
Irish Draught Stout**** Extra Stout (North America)****
Foreign Extra Stout*****

IRISH ALE BREWERS, *Dundalk and Kilkenny.* This is a joint venture between Guinness and the British group Allied Breweries. Its breweries at Dundalk and Kilkenny produce two major ales, the relatively dry Macardle's and the sweeter Smithwick's, and two local smaller local products, the bitter Phoenix and the sweeter Perry's. In addition to the four ales, there is also a Smithwick's Barley Wine.

Macardle's*** Smithwick's** Phoenix*** Perry's**
Smithwick's Barley Wine***

KILLIAN'S, *Enniscorthy.* The increasingly famous Irish Red ale of George Killian Lett, known to drinkers in the U.S. where it is brewed under license by Coors, and in France where it is produced by Pelforth, contains a large proportion of blarney. The picturesque little brewery, in County Wexford, has not made beer since 1956, but continues to make money simply by licensing its former product, known in Ireland as Lett's Ruby Ale.

MURPHY, *Cork.* Producers of the roastiest of the Irish stouts. The only Murphy brand is Stout but the brewery, owned by a consortium of publicans, also produces an ale and a lager under license. In completing the triptych of Irish stout names, Murphy adds yet a third shade of emphasis to the national beer style.

Murphy Stout****½

FRANCE

The nation of great wines also has a brewing tradition dating back to the ancient Gauls. Such a tradition is less surprising in the north than the south, although there have at times been great brewers even in Provence. The two areas of stylistic interest, however, are in the North. Elsewhere, the majority of French beers are uninteresting in character and quality.

The lesser-known of the two brewing areas, and a secret kept too well for their own good by the dour folk of this coal-mining area, is in the northwest, embraced by Région du Nord and Pas-de-Calais, near the city of Lille on the Belgian frontier. There, the influence is Belgian, and the tradition, accordingly, is to produce top-fermenting specialty beers in tiny, craftsman breweries. Until recently, these breweries were closing at a rate that places the would-be consumer of their products in the position of an anthropologist seeking traces of a lost civilization. However, the resurgence of interest in craftsman brewing techniques has brought sufficient attention to one such *bière de garde*, Jenlain, to inspire other brewers to rediscover their traditions. Jenlain is still made by top-fermentation; some of its disciples brew products of a similar character but by the lager method and with a degree of success. Like Jenlain, the other beers in this tradition are inclined to identify themselves outwardly by the use of a corked and wired champagne-style bottle.

The better-known brewing area is in the northeast, in the regions of Lorraine and, more especially, Alsace, and notably around the city of Strasbourg on the German border. Here, the influence, like the language, is German, and the beers are lagers, produced in large breweries for the mass market. Despite this influence, these beers lack the big, malty character of those from across the border. They are inclined to be indecisive and fruity, and this characteristic probably derives from the type of malting barley grown in France.

While the northeast is dotted with scores of tiny breweries, it is the northwest that produces the volume. The French brewing industry is concentrated in a few hands: the diversified food, drink, and bottle-making group BSN owns Kronenbourg and La Meuse and many other products; Union de Brasseries, controlled by an insurance company, has Slavia, 33, and Porter 39; Heineken, of Holland, has Ancre and Mutzig; Artois, of Belgium, has Motte Cordonnier and Vézélise; and there are two other substantial French-owned companies, Pelforth and Fischer/Pêcheur. Mass-marketed beers in France are inclined to have short lagering times of between 12 and 21 days, and to be brewed with the use of up to 30 percent adjuncts.

FISCHER/PÊCHEUR, *Strasbourg*. Both renditions of the word for fisherman are used, in deference to the two languages of Strasbourg. La Belle Strasbourgeoise is another designation used by the company, in the U.S., for a product very similar to its local Fischer Export a light-bodied lager with a good, but a sweetish hop aroma (3.65% w; 4.67% v). The brewery also has a product called Fischer Gold (5.15% w; 6.65% v) with a good aroma, a notably smooth body, and much more character.

Fischer also has an utterly extraordinary product that bears the label of its Adelshoffen subsidiary. This beer, called Adelscott, is brewed from malt kilned with peat, as in the production of Scotch whisky. The result is a very faint hint of the smoky dryness to be found in Scotch (and most assertively evident in the single malts from the island of Islay). Fischer describes this product as "the great innovation in brewing this century" although it might be more dispassionately regarded as a pleasant novelty capitalizing on a French fascination with things Scottish that seems to have thrived ever since the Auld Alliance. In any event, Adelscott Biere au Malt a Whisky (5.2% w; 6.4% v) is a quite agreeable brew. Like all Fischer products, it is lagered for two months.

Fischer Export La Belle Strasbourgeoise** Fischer Gold*** Adelscott****

JENLAIN, *near Valenciennes*. The inspirational *bière de garde* (laying-down beer) is Jenlain, produced in the town of the same name by the Duyck family brewery. It has a full body, a rich fruitiness, and a profound amber colour created exclusively by malts, with no additives. Jenlain (about 5.25% w; 6.5% v) is conditioned for a month and is unpasteurized. It is surely the classic example of the style.

Jenlain*****

KRONENBOURG, *Strasbourg*. Despite now being part of a group, this brewery is still managed by the Hatt family, who founded the company in 1664. Its premium beer in the French market is a relatively full-bodied product called 1664 de Kronenbourg (4.9% w; 6.1% v). A considerably hoppier and more rounded beer, 1664 Reinheitsgebot (4.8% w; 6.0% v), is brewed according to the *Reinheitsgebot* for the German market. In Britain, a rather neutral beer is produced under the name Kronenbourg (4.0% w; 5.0% v) by Harp as a mass-market premium lager. Even in France, the basic Kronenbourg (4.1% w; 5.2% v) is, like most mass-market products, bland. If the Kronenbourg products as a whole have a house character, it is in their inclination to a light fruitiness. In its home market, the company also has a mild lager, Kronenpils (4.0% w; 5.0% v), intended to be served with meals but actually somewhat stronger than a table beer. Given its mildness, the name is not altogether appropriate.

1664 de Kronenbourg*** 1664 Reinheitsgebot***½
Kronenbourg (Britain)* Kronenbourg (France)*½
Kronenpils*½

LUTÈCE, *Paris*. A well-made, all-malt *bière de Paris* called Lutèce (4.4% w; 5.6% v) is produced in the northwestern style by this brewery. Lutèce beer is brewed from Champagne and Gatinais malts, and hops from Burgundy and Alsace. The water, which is rich in calcium carbonate, comes from a rock source underneath Paris. The beer is produced by the lager process and krausened for a secondary fermentation. It is conditioned for, and possesses a lot of finesse. The brewery has been in the hands of the same family since 1918, but only recently have they realized that a traditional product has the capacity to endow the company with new life.

Lutèce****

PELFORTH, *Lille*. This well-known brewery at the heart of the northwestern region is known for its top-fermenting brown beer, Pelforth Brune, which is brewed from a high original gravity (17.3 Balling; about 1069 British; 5.2% w; 6.6% v) and emerges with a full body. Pelforth Brune is pasteurized. The company also produces, by top fermentation, the French-licensed version of George Killian's Irish Red Ale, known as Bière Rousse (16.8 Balling; 1067 British; 5.2% w; 6.6% v). The brewery also produces Dortmunder-style beer with the curious name Reuze (5.5% w; 7.0% v), a premium pilsener-type called Pelforth Pale (4.8% w; 6.0% v), a lager called Pelican Export (4.2% w; 5.3% v), and, by the customary Gallic inversion, the weakest beer in the line, called Bock (3.0% w; 3.8% v).

Pelforth Brune***½ Bière Rousse***½ Reuze***
Pelforth Pale*** Pelican Export**½ Bock*

SAINT LANDELIN, *Crespin.* This descendant of a monastery brewery, located near Valenciennes, produces a fruity *bière de garde* called Reserve Saint Landelin.

Reserve Saint Landelin****

SAINT LÉONARD, *Boulogne.* It looks more like a farmhouse than a brewery, and the workers at the Facon establishment, in the country near Boulogne, still haven't got over the idea that their St. Leonard *bière de garde* (4.5% w; 6.0% v) is actually exported to the U.S. It is imported by the wine company Almaden, and in that local market has to be described as a *brassin* (brew) because it is too strong to be called a beer in California. St. Leonard is an all-malt brew, hopped with Hallertaus and Saaz, and very thoroughly fermented. It is conditioned for six weeks, and pasteurized. The brewery, originally set up by a Belgian to supply British troops during World War I, has been in the hands of the French family Carpentier since 1938. It also produces a range of full-bodied lagers romantically labeled Biere du Pays Boulonnais. These are said to be made with hops, malt, pure water, and passion.

St. Leonard****

33, *Paris.* A name never to be forgotten by thousands of Vietnam veterans. 33 was the beer of the former French colonies, and sometimes still is. It comes in several versions, all inclined to be drier than the Strasbourg beers. The basic beer is called 33 Export (around 4.0% w; 5.0% v). There is also an Extra Dry (5.2% w; 6.6% v) and the full-bodied Record (6.0% w; 7.5% v). Through a takeover in the northwest, the company also has Porter 39 (5.5% w; 6.9% v), a sweetish but characterful beer.

33 Export*½ Extra Dry** Record*** Porter 39***

OTHER
EUROPEAN
COUNTRIES

Switzerland

As one of the earliest centers of Germanic culture, Switzerland has a deeply rooted brewing tradition, although beer plays a less central role in social life than it does in some neighboring countries. By far the greatest number of breweries are in the German-speaking regions, especially around the city of Zürich and in the canton of St. Gallen, although beers of excellent quality can be found everywhere. Swiss beers are protected by a purity law, usually have long lagering times (two or three months), and are, in most cases, unpasteurized.

If the beer-drinker has had cause for complaint in the past, it has been that there was insufficient stylistic variety. The overwhelming majority of Swiss beers are pale lagers of fullish body, very clean palate, and medium hop bitterness. This conformity has, however, been mitigated in recent years by the introduction of several specialty beers.

The strongest beer in the world is one such specialty, launched by Hürlimann, of Zürich. This beer, called Samichlaus (Santa Claus) is produced only once a year. Its original gravity, 25° Balling (1102 British), is less than that of some strong beers, but after a whole year of lagering, it emerges at 11.2% alcohol by volume, which amounts to a mighty 14.0% by weight. Other specialties include altbiers from Warteck of Basel and Cardinal of Fribourg, and weizenbiers from Colanda and from the eponymous brewery in Frauenfeld, of Chur.

Switzerland has about 20 independent breweries, among which are some mavericks that will stay outside the national trade federation. They include Ueli of Basel, Lupo of Hochdorf, Boxer of Romanel-sur-Lausanne, and the local firm in Rothenburg. Some of the larger independents cooperate in a very loosely knit grouping that includes Hürlimann and its Zürich neighbor Löwenbräu. The latter's beers are, in general, much hoppier than those of its far larger and wholly unconnected namesake in Germany.

There are two national giants, the larger of which is the Feldschlösschen group, based in the German-speaking part of the country but also owning Valaisanne in the French-speaking part. Feldschlösschen's Hop-fenperle brand is also known in some export markets. The second largest group, with the Cardinal brand, is SIBRA, based in French-speaking Switzerland. A third grouping links Eichhof in the German-language area with Bellinzona in the Italian-speaking part of the country.

Although the similarities among Swiss beers are more striking than the differences, it is argued that, like the wines of each area, those in the German part of the country are the sweetest, those in the French part the lightest, and those in the Italian part the most assertive.

Austria

In the days, within living memory, when Vienna was the capital of an empire, its lager beers were as famous as its waltzes. In just one swirl of history, with the outbreak of World War I, the last waltz was played for all of that political, economic, and cultural power, and with it went Austria's international influence even as a brewing nation. The country remains a producer of some good beers, but its brewers are no longer household names internationally, nor are they setters of style.

The beers of Austria do, however, have something of a national characteristic in that they are inclined to be very full-bodied, and the best are notably malty, although others are excessively sweet to the point of a cloying fruitiness. Many Austrian beers are all-malt, and brewers using adjuncts are disinclined to be heavy-handed with them. A purity code dating back to Haps-burg times is vague on this score, but bans artificial colourings.

Brewmasters the world over still describe as Viennese the type of malt that has been kilned to produce a reddish-amber beer, but in Austria that style is less revered than it might be. The designation *märzen*, which might be expected to indicate such a beer, and does in Germany, conventionally elicits in Austria merely a deep-golden brew, distinguished only by its maltiness. The brewery where amber Viennese beers were made famous by Anton Dreher's 1841 brew no longer even bears his name, although it is still in operation.

The industry is dominated by two groups, one called simply Bräu AG and the other based on the Gösser brewery, with Stiegl well behind in third position. There are, however, about 30 smaller firms, including two monastery breweries: Augustiner, in Salzburg, and Stiftsbräu Schlägl, north of Linz, on the German and Czech borders. Among the small independents, excellent breweries include Sigl (noted for its weizenbier), in Obertrum, north of Salzburg; Eggenberg (for its Urbock), between Salzburg and Linz; Hofstetten, of St. Martin (brewed for the steelworkers of Linz); Starkenberg, in the

Tyrol; Hubertus at Laa, north of Vienna, on the Czech border; and Kapsreiter, of Schärding, near Linz, on the German border.

BRÄU AG, *Linz*. The giant of the industry, based on the Danube at Linz and owning half a dozen breweries, including the one at Schwechat, near Vienna, where Dreher produced his first lager beer. That particular takeover took place in the late 1970s. The Schwechat brewery has a wide range of products under its own name, among which the best known is probably its hoppy premium beer Steffl Export (4.3% w; 5.4% v).

At the same strength, but from its Zipf brewery, is a notably pale and dry premium beer called Zipfer Urtyp. Each of these bran-names extends to more than one style (ordinary lager, low-cal, Münchner bock, etc.), but in general the Steffl range is hoppy and the Zipfer beers are dry. A third range, Kaiser, comprises sweeter beers. A fourth brand-name, Austria Gold, is applied to a rather nondescript product. Lagering times run from a couple of months for the regular beers to five or six months for the group's two bocks, both pale: Zipfer Stefanibock and Kaiser Festbock (both 5.4% w; 6.75% v).

Steffl Export**½ Zipfer Urtyp**½ Stefanibock***
Festbock**½

GÖSSER, *Leoben*. In Styria, a region that gives its name to a famous hop (though the variety is today more likely to be harvested across the border in Yugoslavia). In fact, Gösser beers are typically Austrian in their malty fullness. The company's products include Gösser Märzen (3.6% w; 4.5% v), described as being of the Vienna type, although it is pale, and lagered for two months; a much hoppier Spezial (4.2% w; 5.25% v) that is lagered for ten weeks; a rather delicate Pils (3.6% w; 4.5% v) lagered for eight or nine weeks; a very unusual, sweet and malty monastery brew called Stiftsbräu (2.9% w; 3.6% v), reddish and dark, that is lagered for three weeks. This product is named after the Renaissance Benedictine abbey that adjoins the brewery and now houses a beer museum. Like some other Austrian breweries, Gösser also produces a dark sweet beer described as a bock but with a low alcohol content for such a designation. This Dunkler Bock has a suitably high original gravity (16° Balling; 4.0% w; 5.0% v) and with only one month of lagering. A pale counterpart, Heller Bock (5.3% w; 6.6% v) has the same gravity and more than four months of lagering.

Marzen**½ Spezial*** Pils** Stiftsbräu***
Dunkler Bock*½ Heller Bock***

OTTAKRINGER HARMER, *Vienna*. A family-owned brewery, but big enough to export to at least some distant markets. The brewery uses the name Goldfassl on its typically sweetish Pils and Spezial.

Goldfassl Pils**½ Goldfassl Spezial***

REININGHAUS, *Graz.* A sizable brewery in an important city, and part of the same Styrian group as Gösser. Reininghaus produces beers under its own name, but is better known for the Puntigam label. Its products include one of the more characterful examples of the Austrian-type Märzen (4.0% w; 5.0% v) lagered for eight weeks; a premium lager called Panther (4.4% w; 5.4% v) lagered for ten weeks and a very mild Pils (4.1% w; 5.1% v) lagered for ten weeks; a malty Export (4.0% w; 5.0% v) lagered for eight weeks; a very sweet dark Dunkler Bock (4.5% w; 5.6% v) lagered for ten weeks; and a drier pale Heller Bock (5.5% w; 6.9% v) lagered for fifteen weeks.

Puntigam Märzen*** ½ Panther** Pils** ½ Export** ½
Dunkler Bock*** Heller Bock*** ½

STIEGL, *Salzburg.* In a city known for its beer-halls, Stiegl is a significant regional brewery. It also exports a range of beers to the U.S., although they possibly resemble each other more than their stylistic designations would suggest. The company's basic beer, Goldbräu (4.0% w; 5.0% v), lagered for two months, and the Spezial (4.3% w; 5.4% v), lagered for three months, are both very sweet; the latter is quite characterful, with an unusual depth of colour . The brewery has an extremely full-bodied Pils (4.3% w; 5.4% v) that is lagered for three months and has a big bitterness, and a similarly hoppy but less malty product called Columbus (4.3% w; 5.4% v) that is lagered for three months. Its münchner-style dark beer has a full body, three months of lagering, and the curious brand-name Paracelsus (3.5% w; 4.4% v).

Goldbräu** Spezial*** Pils*** Columbus** ½ Paracelsus** ½

Eastern Europe

East Germany (p.28) and Czechoslovakia (p.24-27) have their own special traditions, but all of the countries of eastern Europe have brewing industries of one scale or another. For reasons both of climate and cultural background, those with a brewing tradition are Poland, to a lesser extent Hungary, and marginally the Soviet Union (though, because of its large population, one of the world's biggest producers of beer). Elsewhere in the east, some perfectly drinkable beers may be found, sometimes brewed with Czech advice, but wine is the main drink.

POLAND

The Slavic brewing tradition in Poland is most evident in the Zywiec/Krakus beers, in the foothills of the Tatra mountains (whence they take their water), near Cracow. They sometimes seem to lack life, but these beers manifest in their refractive colour and emphatic hoppiness some of the characteristics of their Czech neighbors. In the important brewing city of Wroclaw (formerly Breslau) and around Gdansk (Danzig), the Slavic influence is overlaid by the Prussian. Danzig, noted for its famous liqueur Goldwasser, was also once known for a type of dark beer brewed with rose hips. An extract with which to home-brew this beer is still available locally. Strong, but bottom-fermenting, "porter" is still brewed in Poland, and many of the local pilsener-type beers are all-malt and unpasteurized.

HUNGARY

The brewing tradition of Hungary derives from the Austro-Hungarian empire. The great Viennese brewer Anton Dreher built the most famous brewery in Hungary in 1854. By happy coincidence, the quarrying of stone to build Buda's twin town of Pest had left enormous rock caverns that were ideal for the lagering of beer. The brand-name Rocky Cellar is still used for the brewery's premium pilsener-style beer. A strong lager is also produced under the name Hungaria (6.0% w; 7.5% v), and there is a marginally bottom-fermenting "porter". There are three or four breweries in other parts of Hungary, living in peaceful coexistence with the producers of Bull's Blood and Tokay, apricot brandy and Borovicka gin.

THE SOVIET UNION

In a tradition reminiscent of ancient Egypt's brewing methods, the Russians produce a beery alcoholic drink by the fermentation of bread. This drink, which is sometimes found in other parts of the world and even as a home-brew in the U.S., is known as kvass. Russia also has a huge production of more conventional beers, often brewed with technical assistance from the Czechs. Despite this, both quality and availability are erratic. These beers are all lagers, but travelers have reported sightings of ales produced on a tiny local scale. The state encourages the drinking of beer as a more temperate alternative to spirits (the same is true in Mexico, although in both countries the two are apt to go hand in hand). In Russia, as in Poland, there is an intense cultural devotion to vodka, the history of which straddles these two great Slavic nations.

Southern Europe

The warm south grows grapes, and its traditions are in wine-making, but it still has some acceptable lager beers and one tiny country, Malta, even has ales.

SPAIN AND PORTUGAL

In recent years an increasingly well-known name, San Miguel has drawn attention to the beers of Spain, at least among drinkers with a European perspective. San Miguel has breweries at Lerida, Malaga, and Burgos but it is not, in fact, Spanish. The beer has been produced in Spain since 1957, but San Miguel is based in a former Spanish colony, the Philippines, where it has been brewing since 1890. The basic San Miguel beer is a well-made pilsener-style of 80 percent malt, with a clean palate, and a crisp, underlying hop bitterness. The Spanish version (4.3% w; 5.4% v) is fractionally stronger in alcohol than the Far Eastern products. It is also lagered for two months, whereas they are lagered for one. The Spanish breweries of San Miguel also have a full-bodied and well-hopped premium product called Selecta XV (5.2% w; 6.5% v) that is lagered for two months but, unlike the parent company, they don't produce a dark münchner type. Although San Miguel is surely the best-known brewery in Spain, Aguila has larger sales, and there are several other local firms.

ITALY

It is easy to be unaware just how strong the Germanic and Austrian influence is in northern Italy, but that probably explains the fact that some of the country's beers are quite big in body and others are notably hoppy. The Austrian connection has special dimension in the city of Trieste, the principal port of the Hapsburg empire and the place where the great Viennese brewer Anton Dreher established an outpost in 1868. In Austria, there is no longer a brewing company called Dreher, but in Italy there still is, albeit jointly controlled by Heineken of Holland and Whitbread of Britain. The other major Italian brewers are Peroni, Wührer, Prinz Bräu, Poretti, and Moretti. The latter produces a full-bodied and well-balanced pilsener-type beer that has found some favour beyond Italy.

YUGOSLAVIA

An area of Austrian brewing influence in the past, and still an important hop-growing nation. The principal region of cultivation is Slovenia, which is also the home of the well-known Union beers, quite full-bodied and hoppy, with an almost brandy-like assertiveness. Brands are inclined to be available on a regional basis, and to become less hoppy and more full-bodied the further the drinker ventures south. In the course of travelling south, beer becomes less important than wine. South of Zagreb, the town of Karlovac gives its name to a popular beer, as does Nikšić, in Montenegro.

GREECE

A pure beer law introduced to coincide with Greece's entry into the European Economic Community (and therefore protect the handful of local brewers against mass-market imported beers) promised to add a malty flavour to a country whose indigenous character is grapy, not to mention resinous. However, this was followed by the election of a government that talked of quitting the Community, leaving the politics of beer in a state of confusion. Beer was initially popularized in Greece to suit the tourist trade, and the pace was set by a product cryptically called Fix (from Fuchs, the name of the German brewer), but the country has so far produced nothing of great interest. Cyprus has a characterful lager called Keo.

MALTA

Notable as the only nation in this part of the world to produce ales. Not only are they produced there, but more ale than lager is imbibed. Two of the ales, Brewer's Choice (4.0% w; 5.0% v) and Blue Label (3.2% w; 4.0% v) are decidedly English in colour and style, bearing witness to the Colonial origins of these habits, which have since also been reinforced by British tourists. A third ale, Hop Leaf (3.2% w; 4.0% v) has a golden colour that is quite coincidentally reminiscent of its Canadian counterparts. It is unlike them in palate, however, manifesting less estery fruitiness and far more hop character, true to its name. All three benefit from slow and caring brewhouse procedures; a complex blend of several species of English whole hops is used, the ales are top-fermented in open tanks, and all three are then both warm- and cold-conditioned, gaining not only a significant flavour maturation but also stability. They are then pasteurized and served either from the bottle or under pressure, since cask-conditioning is not felt to be feasible in such a hot climate and in the absence of British-style pub cellars. A genuine milk stout (3.5% w; 4.4% v) and a well-made, award-winning lager called Cisk (3.6% w; 4.5% v) are also produced. The brewery, the only one on the island, is called Simonds Farsons Cisk. It is locally owned, although the British company Courage has a minority stake.

CANADA

It is widely believed in North America, and oft repeated with great confidence, that Canadian beers are substantially more potent than those of the U.S. This is a myth. They are, indeed, stronger, but only slightly. It is true that in the U.S. light beers, and most cheap brands, are pretty low in alcohol, but most of the better-known regular brands have between 3.5 percent and 4.0 percent by weight. All of the main Canadian brands have 4.0 percent. The exaggeration of this small distinction arises because the two countries use different systems for expressing the strength of their beers. A brew of 4.0 percent *by weight* (the system used in the U.S.) has 5.0 percent *by volume* (the scale employed in Canada). Hence the notion that Canada has five percent beers. Four and five percent can mean the same thing depending on which side of the border you stand.

Almost all Canadian beers, whether lagers, ales, or porters, have this potency of 4.0 percent (or 5.0 percent) and the only definite exception is the single strong brand of each of the major brewers with around 5.0 percent by weight, 6.25 by volume, or fractionally more. In the U.S., Canadian ales have become well known. They certainly represent a notable regional tradition, though in style they are of the restrained, fruity, pale style typically found on the eastern seaboard of North America on both sides of the border. Ale is the dominant beer style in Quebec, and has about half the market in Ontario, though it is losing popularity there, on the grounds of being old-fashioned. (In the U.S., ales are gaining popularity as drinkers turn toward tradition in search of more interesting products.)

In their traditional regions, Canadian ales are all genuinely made, by top-fermentation, though this is not always the case elsewhere. Nationally, there are scores of beer brands but the overwhelming majority belong to three groups, so the extent of choice is to some extent illusory. To the extent that each of the national groups has a house character, Carling's products are inclined to be light, fruity and sweet; Labatt's are in some cases yet sweeter, and often rather malty; and Molson's are drier in a way that is both yeasty and hoppy. The smaller Moosehead brewery produces relatively big, hoppy beers, in line with local taste in the Maritime provinces where it is based. The activities of the three or four other small breweries have been subject to much change in recent years. In a wild, sprawling country that has always attracted adventurous business people, the brewing industry has not been exempt from this rather entrepreneurial approach.

The most colourful of the brewing entrepreneurs, "Uncle Ben" Ginter, has a production of somewhat erratic quality at his plant in Red Deer, Alberta. His former plant at Prince George, British Columbia, has been sold to another entrepreneur, and operates under the name Old Fort, producing a couple of pilsener-type beers: a robust Pacific Gold and a more mellow Yukon Gold, both lagered for five weeks. Another small company, Northern Breweries, sprung from Carling through divestment to employees. The only outside incursion has been from Henninger, of Germany, whose small plant in Hamilton, Ontario, has now been taken over by Heineken/Amstel, of Holland.

CARLING, *Toronto.* Internationally, the best-known of the Canadian brewers, largely as a result of the activities of a former owner who entered the U.S. and British markets, although the company subsequently withdrew from both. The familiar Carling Black Label brand is, in the U.S., in the hands of Heileman, and in Britain is licensed to Bass, whose Toby ale is, in return, in the portfolio of the Canadian brewer. Despite its withdrawals from the international scene, the Canadian company (full name: Carling O'Keefe) still owns the tiny Beamish and Crawford brewery in Cork, Ireland. By happy coincidence, the original Mr. O'Keefe came from County Cork. Carling O'Keefe is now part of the South African-based Rothmans group.

In Canada, the Carling Black Label brand is no longer preeminent, and the company's rather sweeter Old Vienna has superseded it in popularity. The principal top-fermenting brand is O'Keefe Ale, fruity and carbonic, with a rather thin finish. Similar products are produced in branch breweries under the Dow name and the once-famous Black Horse and Red Cap brands. A more characterful Buckeye Ontario Special Ale is yet fruitier, as well as having a better hop character. There is a pleasant Cream Porter under the Dow label, and a similar product called Champlain. These brews are all in the range of 4.0 percent alcohol by weight, 5.0 percent by volume. Beyond that range is a stronger lager called Extra Old Stock; the principal product in this category is a full-bodied but dry Carlsberg Gold (5.2% w; 6.5% v).

Carling Black Label*½ Old Vienna*½ O'Keefe Ale** Buckeye*** Dow Porter** Carlsberg Gold**½

LABATT, *London, Ontario.* International expansion, albeit on a lesser scale, was until recently part of Labatt's policy but this company, too, has withdrawn from some foreign activities. The controlling interest is in the hands of two members of the Bronfman family, dynastically (though not commercially) linked to the owners of Seagrams, the world's biggest drinks group.

The company's best-known product, highly regarded in Canada, is Labatt's Pilsener Beer, popularly known simply as Blue after the colour of its label. Blue has a surprisingly hoppy nose, given the pronounced sweetness of its palate, and a soft body. Labatt has quite a range of lagers, including the maltier Gold Keg, a dryish Crystal, a version of Skol that has some warm conditioning, a low-alcohol beer called Cool Spring (3.2% w; 4.0% v) that has a markedly hoppy nose, and a licensed Budweiser (4.0% w; 5.0% v). The company also produces a version of Guinness, under license, though with less success in terms of fidelity to palate, and it has an unmemorable Velvet Cream Porter. Its principal ale, Labatt 50, has an aromatic palate, and the company also has an IPA. This last turns out, disappointingly, to be an ale of the North American golden type, but it has a good earthy hop bouquet and a full, all-malt body. In the upper strength division, Labatt has its well-regarded Extra Stock Malt Liquor, which is best appreciated on draught. Like its competitors, the company also uses a wide variety of more local brand-names.

Labatt's "Blue"*** Gold Keg* Crystal* Skol** Cool Spring** Budweiser** Guinness*** Porter* ½ Labatt 50** IPA*** ½ Extra Stock***

MOLSON, *Quebec*. A deeply rooted company, in which the Molson family has been involved since its foundation in 1786. Today, it is probably by a whisker the largest of Canada's big three brewing companies, as well as having diversified into lumber and other industries. It is also the world's second-largest exporter of beers to the U.S., after Heineken of Holland.

Although the Canadian big three all have similar approaches to brewing, Molson probably take the most pains to impart quality and identity to its products. It is particularly well known for its ales. Its basic ale, Molson Golden, is light, smooth, and very much for the beginner (in the local French-speaking market, the counterpart is Laurentide Ale.) Its Export (marketed in the U.S. simply as Molson Ale) has the same strength, but markedly more body, a typically Canadian aromatic fruitiness (almost citric) and an emphatic hop character. It is definitely the hoppiest of the big-selling Canadian ales, for what that distinction is worth. Among the lesser-known products, Stock Ale (still at 4.0% w; 5.0% v) has much more hop character, and an all-malt body. The most interesting of all Molson's products has the strange name Brador, an ugly contraction of Brassée d'Or (5.0% w; 6.25% v) and a top-fermenting counterpart to a malt liquor. Having been hopped as an ale and fermented with a top yeast, Brador has a palate quite different from the malt liquors it superficially resembles. It is in this respect a unique product. In Newfoundland, Molson also has a bottom-fermenting malt liquor, misleadingly described as IPA. Another of its regional lagers is, curiously named India Beer. The company's basic lager is called Molson Canadian (4.0% w; 5.0% v). It is quite full-bodied, with a complex palate and a Hallertau nose. In some markets, there is also a lighter weight lager called Molson Diamond (4.0% w; 5.0% v). Not surprisingly, this is drier, with the hop coming through more clearly. A very hoppy, all-Hallertau lager misleadingly called Molson Oktoberfest is also available in some markets. Another local product, Molson Porter, which emanates from the brewery at Barrie, Ontario, is Canada's most authentic example of this style. Other porters and stouts are produced by Molson elsewhere in Canada.

Molson Golden** Molson (Export) Ale***
Molson Stock Ale***½ Brador**** Molson Diamond**
Molson Canadian**½ Molson Oktoberfest***
Molson Porter***

MOOSEHEAD, *Nova Scotia and New Brunswick.* The appeal of Moosehead beer in the U.S. has brought considerable growth in sales to this provincial company, with its two breweries in remote locations. The colourful name and frontierish source no doubt create a romantic appeal, but the products do have a hint of character to match. The hardier nature of beers from this part of Canada is evident in both their hop character and body, although the style is still emphatically North American rather than European. Indeed, the Moosehead product marketed in the U.S., under the label Canadian Lager, is fractionally lighter than the company's local brand, Alpine. Both, though, are relatively full-bodied and smooth. Moosehead also has a typically Canadian ale, with some of the characteristic sweetness, called Export (4.0% w; 5.0% v); a drier Pale Ale (4.0% w; 5.0% v); and a slightly darker and more character-ful Ten Penny Old Stock Ale (4.25% w; 5.3% v). All of its products are hopped three times with blends that include Czech varieties for aroma. The company also has a London (sic) Stout.

Moosehead Canadian Lager**½ Alpine Lager Beer***
Export Ale** Pale Ale**½ Ten Penny Stock Ale***½
London Stout**

THE
UNITED STATES

When the U.S. beer drinker is in a mood to be critical, the complaints are often misdirected. The fundamental criticism of U.S. beers is not that they are especially weak, which they are not (though it can sometimes be hard to find a strong one). Nor is it that they are a mess of additives (although some are). It is that they lack variety.

The overwhelming majority of beers produced in the U.S. are of but one style: they are pale lager beers vaguely of the pilsener style but lighter in body, notably lacking hop character, and generally bland in palate. They do not all taste exactly the same but the differences between them are often of minor consequence.

QUALITY DESIGNATIONS

A typical U.S. brewery produces three or four basic beers, all pale lagers, but differing in quality. The distinctions are likely to lie in the amount of barley malt used, the varieties of hop employed, and the time taken for maturation. Differences in alcohol content are generally less significant, although the cheapest beer may have only 3.2 percent by weight, while the most expensive might have 4.2 percent. In ascending order of quality, brewers regard their products as *price, regular, premium,* and *super-premium.* Only the latter two designations are likely to find their way to the labels.

THE WEST COAST

It is more than coincidence that the seedbed of the wine renaissance in the U.S. should also have given rise to the new appreciation of serious beers. It was the success of the boutique wineries in northern California that helped encourage the establishment of the first new small breweries there in the late 1970s.

The climate is economically and sociologically right, too. The interest in wine and beer in the West is part of a broader enthusiasm for gastronomy, itself made possible by the prosperity of California. West Coast wine writers like Robert Lawrence Balzer and Robert Finigan have done good work in furthering serious interest in beer.

ANCHOR STEAM, *San Francisco, California.* The only beer made by a procedure that is indigenous to the U.S. As the last surviving brewery to use this method, Anchor has become the protector of the style, notwithstanding some clumsy attempts at imitation. As the definitive example, Anchor Steam Beer is without question a world classic.

Contrary to a widely held belief, it is not an ale. It is a hybrid. Steam Beer is made with lager yeasts, but fermented at ale temperatures in long, shallow pan-like vessels called clarifiers. This method is said to have been developed in the San Francisco Bay area during the 1890s, at a time when lager-brewing was fashionable but difficult to carry out in Californian temperatures. The beer is warm-conditioned and krausened, and these procedures endow it with a lively head. Allegedly, the pressure released when the wooden casks were tapped was, in times past, dubbed steam; hence the name of the product. This may be apocryphal, since in the last half of the 19th century many breweries proudly proclaimed that they used steam power. The Anchor Brewery was about to close in 1965 when it was rescued by a patron, Fritz Maytag of the washing machine family, who simply liked the beer and didn't want to see it vanish. At the time, Anchor Steam had a reputation for inconsistency in its product, of which it brewed only 600 barrels a year. Today, its consistency and quality are outstanding, and about 30,000 barrels are produced. With no background in the industry, Maytag learned to brew through experience and study, and has become one of the best-respected practitioners of the art in the U.S. In the late 1970s, he went to Germany and bought equipment, and reconstructed his little brewery in new premises. Anchor Steam is now one of the best-equipped and most well-run breweries in the country.

All Anchor products products are made wholly with barley malt, whole hops are used, and flash pasteurization is employed in preference to tunnel pasteurization. Anchor Steam Beer itself (3.8% w; 4.75% v) has a copper colour, firm body, and excellent hop character (the species is Northern Brewer) in both the palate and the nose. The brewery has recently installed a new facility for top fermentation, and Anchor Porter (4.5% w; 5.6% v), a slightly sweet interpretation of the style, gains authenticity in its move from bottom to top fermentation. Anchor makes a different Christmas Ale each year (4.5% w; 5.6% v). To date, these top-fermenting ales have been dry-hopped with Cascade hops, and have had enormous hop bitterness.

Anchor Steam Beer***** Anchor Porter*** Christmas Ale****

BLITZ-WEINHARD, *Portland, Oregon.* The leader of the new wave of super-premium beers with its Henry Weinhard's Private Reserve (3.7% w; 4.6% v), a product only available in the West and Southwest and in Colorado, and the inspiration of one or two conspicuous imitators. The defining characteristic of Henry's is its delicate use of Cascades, especially as a finishing hop. They are lightly used in the copper, but great emphasis is given to bouquet. Henry's has a firm, clean, fairly light body. It is brewed exclusively from two-row barley, employs 80 percent malt, and is fermented for two weeks and lagered for four. The brewery's regular beer, known simply as Blitz, is light and clean in the Western style, although less anemic than some of its neighbors. Blitz-Weinhard also produces a malt liquor under the curious name of Olde English 800 (6.0% w; 7.5% v), the strongest beer in the U.S.

The company has been a leader of the trend toward more informative advertising of beer, especially in its campaign for Henry's. Blitz-Weinhard has retained its own personality and its own products as a regional brewer, despite having been acquired by Pabst. The plant, close to the center of Portland, has a magnificent galleried brewhouse.

Henry Weinhard's Private Reserve*** Blitz**
Olde English 800*½

BOULDER BREWERY, *Boulder, Colorado.* A boutique brewery that released its first commercial products in the spring of 1980. Boulder brews three very well-made products: a Stout, a Porter, and a Bitter ale (each about 5.5% w; 6.8% v). All are produced by top-fermentation and bottle-conditioned. The brewery is also considering producing a lighter and paler ale for summer. Boulder Bitter has a fruity nose, an aperitif dryness, and a roundness of body that is malty without being at all heavy. Boulder Porter is well-balanced, with a gentle roastiness and some estery dryness. Boulder Stout has a markedly fuller body, with just a hint of sweetness in the aftertaste.

This tiny, 600-barrel brewery is supplied with whole Cascade and Hallertau hops by its only local competitor, the Coors Brewery, which also supplies pale malts, although crystal and black malts and roasted barley are bought elsewhere. Boulder began operation in a goathouse, but now has a tiny well-designed plant constructed by the brewmaster and partners. They even drilled their own well, and do not change the water that issues from it. Should they have any technical problems, they are well-equipped to cope: one partner is an engineer and the other two are physicists.

Boulder Bitter*** ½ Boulder Porter**½ Boulder Stout*½

CARTWRIGHT, *Portland, Oregon.* Having run a winery, Chuck Coury decided to try his hand at commercial brewing. He named his boutique brewery after his wife, Shirley Cartwright, and marketed his first beer in late 1980. Early samples gave evidence of some technical problems, but a much more interesting product was available by the middle of 1981. Cartwright Portland Beer (just under 4.0% w; 5.0% v) has the characteristics of an ale and is bottle-conditioned, but is fermented with a lager yeast. It is a big beer with a lot of mouth, but its fullness of body is mitigated by a substantial bitterness. Its ale character derives from fermentation at relatively high temperatures and by warm-conditioning.

Cartwright Portland Beer* ½

COORS, *Golden, Colorado*. The biggest single-plant brewery in the world, with a capacity of 15 million barrels. In light of its size, it is remarkable that Coors became fashionable during the 1970s among people who apparently thought it was a funky little brewery up in the mountains. This illusion grew from the fact that for many years Coors beer (3.5% w; 4.3% v) was available only in the Rocky Mountain states. Coors' regional market is thinly populated, but it spreads for thousands of square miles and has not been especially well penetrated by the national giants. Only when the company began to reveal its own status as a national giant by marketing itself more aggressively, and when the Rightist views of Adolph Coors became more widely known, did the beer lose its radical chic in California and New York. The chic obscured the fact that Coors is the ultimate U.S. beer in terms of its light, clean, refreshing character. When the company launched a Coors Light, it was rather like Volkswagen announcing that it had added a small car to its range.

The clean, floral palate of Coors' beers derives in part from the extremely high quality of the hops and malt used and from the immense care taken in production, but it also owes much to the absence of pasteurization. Coors pioneered the use of very fine filtration, which, by avoiding the need for pasteurization, contributes greatly to the remarkably fresh taste of Coors' canned and bottled beers.

After many years as a one-product company, Coors has recently launched two other new products on a limited scale. One is a super-premium beer called Herman Joseph's, with a pronounced character of Hallertau hops in both the bouquet and the palate. The other is an Irish Red Ale, a much more unusual venture, considering Coors' regular products. Irish Red Ale is brewed under license from the George Killian Lett company. This brewery in Ireland has not produced any beer of its own for a quarter of a century, but has a similar licensing agreement with Pelforth in France (see p. 93). The Coors-brewed version of this Irish Red has an excellent colour a yeasty, fluffy body, and a distinctive malt character.

Coors** ½ Herman Joseph's** ½ Irish Red Ale***

DE BAKKER, *Marin County, California.* When a panel of wine-tasters sampled De Bakker Pale Ale in a blindfold appraisal at San Francisco's Washington Square Bar and Grill, in 1980, they rated it the best ale on the West Coast. It is a remarkably complex ale (4.1% w; 5.2% v), very well-balanced and nutty, with a notably small bead. De Bakker also produces a Porter (4.1% w; 5.2% v), which is dry and clean, with a pronounced character of roasted malt. Both beers are bottle-conditioned. Whole Cluster and Cascade hops are used, and the copper is heated by direct fire. Brewer-owner Tom De Bakker, a firefighter by trade, had been a home-brewer for ten years before marketing his first commercial beer in 1979. During those years, he had planned his brewery and worked to perfect his product. By the middle of 1981, his brewery was in the black, and he was considering giving up his work as a firefighter.

De Bakker Pale Ale*** Porter** ½

NEW ALBION, *Sonoma, California.* The first boutique brewery in the U.S. Like most of those that followed, its principal product is a top-fermenting ale in what might be regarded as the English style. Among these various boutique products, New Albion Ale (1055; 4.1% w; 5.2% v) is the truest to the model in its hoppy bitterness and well-attenuated body. New Albion also pioneered porters and stouts as a boutique line. Its Porter (1055; 4.1% w; 5.2% v) has the big bitterness of Bullion hops, and its Stout (1055; 4.1% w; 5.2% v) has pronounced character of highly roasted black malt. The inspiration for these distinctive bottle-conditioned brews was the British beer that co-owner Jack McAuliffe drank when he was stationed in Scotland with the U.S. Navy. When he left the service, McAuliffe took up home-brewing, and in 1976 went into commercial production with the help of a couple of friends (one of them, Suzy Stern, still works as co-brewer). New Albion is planning to move to a new brewery, and has engaged a well-known distributor, Boles, with a view to a wider marketing of its products.

New Albion Ale*** Porter*** Stout** ½

OLYMPIA, *Olympia, Washington.* "It's the water," says the slogan of the Olympia brewery, which is in the town of the same name. Olympia heavily promotes its use of water from artesian springs at nearby Tumwater Falls, and its beers have an appropriately light, clean taste in the typical Western style. The regular Olympia (3.5% w; 4.3% v) is light, but its Olympia Gold is even lighter. Olympia also produces a caramel-tasting Dark, and imports a product under the Grenzquell label from the Bavaria St. Pauli brewery of Hamburg.

Olympia*

RAINIER, *Seattle, Washington.* Rainier Ale, popularly known as The Green Death, is famous among the beer-drinkers of the West and enjoys a special reputation in northern California, where they like their beers to be a little different. The nickname derives from the green label and the alcohol content (5.8% w; 7.25% v). Ironically, except in specially licensed outlets, Rainier Ale has to be sold at 4.0 percent in its home state. Rainier represents a remarkably successful attempt to produce a beer with ale character-istics by bottom-fermentation. The secret lies in the use of very high fermenting temperatures and a distinctive yeast, which together produce a winy character to balance the maltiness of this big, copper-coloured brew.

All of the other long-established ales in the U.S. are in the East. How did Rainier come to be in the West? The answer is that, at various stages, the brewery was under the ownership of the Canadian companies Sick's and Molson, and both considered an ale to be a natural part of the portfolio. Although Rainier is now part of the Heileman group, it has retained its own character. The company also has a fairly full-bodied lager called Rainier Beer.

Rainier Ale**** Rainier Beer*

RIVER CITY, *Sacramento, California.* Ex-Schlitz brewer James Schlueter founded this boutique brewery with his wife Chris Hoover in 1980–81. While the tendency has been for the boutiques to produce ales, he thought small-scale brewing offered the perfect opportunity to make a tradi-tional lager. The brewery's highly distinctive River City Gold (3.9% w; 4.8% v) is an all-malt brew with the somewhat tannic firmness of Tettnang hops and some fruitiness deriving from the yeast strain. It is matured for five weeks and, most unusually for a lager, dry-hopped. Although it is a bottled product, it is not pasteurized; its traditional-ism is uncompromising. River City Gold is much bigger and more characterful than typical U.S. lagers.

River City Gold***

SIERRA NEVADA, *Chico, California.* The most ambitious of the West Coast boutiques, this brewery has established itself with a capacity of 1,500 barrels. Its principal product is a Pale Ale (3.9% w; 4.8% v), a very well-balanced and eminently drinkable bottle-conditioned ale with a floral bouquet and a smooth, fruity, malty body. At a similar strength, Sierra Nevada produces a well-attenuated hoppy Porter with a good roasted-malt character, and the brewery is experimenting with a strongish stout. Both of the founding partners were originally home-brewers, and one previously owned a shop selling equipment and supplies to home brewers and wine-makers.

Pale Ale***

THE MIDWEST

Three circumstances contrived to make the Midwest the heartland of U.S. brewing from the middle of the 19th century. This part of the country was settled mainly by Northern Europeans, especially Germans, fleeing from the privations of the Old World during the 1840s. These immigrants brought with them a new technique in brewing, the lager method, that had recently been perfected in the German-speaking world. In order to brew lager beer, they needed ice, and the cold winters and Great Lakes of the Midwest provided plenty of that. It is also the case that the grain belt of the Midwest encouraged the use of corn as a raw material in the production of beer; whether that was a good thing is open to question.

ANHEUSER-BUSCH, *St. Louis, Missouri.* What is now the world's biggest brewing company faced collapse twice in the 1850s before it was bought in 1860 by Eberhard Anheuser, a creditor whose daughter married a brewers' supplier named Adolphus Busch. A Busch still heads the company, but the family name is given only to the company's basic beer. It was Adolphus Busch's Czechoslovakian-inspired Budweiser premium beer, launched in 1876 as a brew to transcend regional tastes, that was to become the world's biggest-selling brand. It is some measure of Budweiser's success that this world-beating sale is largely achieved within the U.S. market. Some recent overseas adventures of Budweiser may prove interesting, but the major U.S. beer brands can hardly be called international competitors.

    The defining characteristic of Budweiser is a unique, delicate fruitiness deriving from "apple" esters. Great care is taken to produce a beer with this distinctive but subtle character by a brewing company that has a fierce pride in its traditionalism. To Europeans, the company's proud boast concerning its choice of adjunct strikes a strange note, but it does make some sense in the U.S. While European brewers are inclined to be reticent about their use of adjuncts, Budweiser proudly proclaims its choice of rice in preference to the corn widely used by other brewers. It is pointed out that rice is generally more expensive than corn, and the brewery claims that it "contributes to the snappy taste, clarity, and brilliance" of the beer. A greater reason for pride, though it is not publicized, is the care taken in hopping. Eight or nine varieties of whole hops are used, including several imported species, in a three-stage procedure. In light of the care taken with the blend of hops, it could be argued that the end result is just a mite too delicate. The beer is krausened, lagered for a minimum of three weeks, and clarified by being passed over a bed of beechwood chips. The beechwood attracts yeast particles, and this time-consuming method of fining is very much a U.S. tradition, dating back to the 1860s and now a distinctive feature of this brewing company's methods. Anheuser-Busch is a proponent of natural brewing, and eschews the use of additives. The company uses tannin to prevent a chill haze, but removes all but tiny traces that occur naturally in hops and grains.

Budweiser (3.9% w; 4.8% v) is made with 70 percent malt. Michelob (3.9% w; 4.8% v), the original super-premium beer, uses 80 percent malt (all from two-row barley) and employs only imported hops. It is brewed from a higher original gravity than is Bud and is lagered for a minimum of 32 days. Michelob has a characteristically smooth, malty palate. The company produces a sweetish Classic Dark and several light beers, and imports a rather mild all-malt beer from Würzburger Hofbrau in Germany.

Busch* ½ Budweiser** ½ Michelob** ½ Würzburger** ½

COLD SPRING, *Cold Spring, Minnesota.* "It's the water that made Cold Spring Export," says the slogan for this small brewery's super-premium brand. The water is also sold by the bottle, and comes from the spring itself, which flows into a creek alongside the brewery complete with mallards nesting among the watercress.

Cold Spring Export (4.2% w; 5.25% v) is an 85 percent malt beer, notably full-bodied and with a hint of Cascade hops. The brewery also produces a similar but milder beer called Gemeinde (the German word for community) for the Amana religious colonies in Iowa. Another Amana beer called Colonie, still fairly malty but slightly lighter, resembles the brewery's own premium beer Kegelbrau (4.0% w; 5.0% v). The Amana beers are said to be brewed to old community recipes. Cold Spring also produces a regular beer and a similar product called Fox DeLuxe (both 3.6% w; 4.1% v).

Cold Spring Export** Gemeinde* ½

GEYER, *Frankenmuth, Michigan.* The smallest of the old-established breweries in the U.S., with an output of only about 4,000 barrels a year, and one of the most unusual in that its principal product is a copper-coloured Bavarian Dark beer. This surprisingly dry beer, brewed with Vienna malts, has a light palate that seems to gain character with the drinking. A slightly paler seasonal Oktoberfest and a regular beer are also produced, all under the Frankenmuth Bavarian label. A lighter but hoppier regular beer is called Geyer. The beers, all produced by a 72-year-old brewmaster, are fermented in open iron tanks and are krausened (all about 4.2% w; 5.25% v). The brewery, which welcomes visitors, is a county historical site. "She's small, she's beautiful, and she's precious," says company president Richard Brozovic.

Frankenmuth Bavarian (Dark)*** Frankenmuth Bavarian** Geyer**

HEILEMAN, *La Crosse, Wisconsin*. The spritzy, krausened, super-premium Special Export (3.9% w; 4.8% v), lightened with rice and with a fragrant balance between German Spalt and domestic Hallertau, is helping make Heileman a national name. The same brewery's fuller-bodied and sweeter Old Style also enjoys some popularity, and has notably compensated for the astonishing lack of a local beer in Chicago. "From God's Country," explain the advertisements, but Heileman's increasing omnipresence may have more to do with takeovers of breweries in other states, such as Washington and Florida (not to mention the U.S. interests of the Canadian brewer Carling) than with divine connections.

Special Export** Old Style* ½

HUBER, *Monroe, Wisconsin*. This quality-conscious small company, having already set an example to its peers with the super-premium Augsburger, is now reviving Van Merritt, a Midwestern favourite that vanished with the closure of the related Peter Hand brewery in Chicago. There are even plans for a Huber-produced weissbier. The new Van Merritt is intended to be an even hoppier brother brew to Augsburger, and is inspired by the success of that distinctive product. Augsburger is an old-established brand that gained greatly in complexity after a chance meeting with a German brewmaster in 1976 led proprietor Fred Huber to experiment with Spalt hops, which are not widely used in the U.S.

Augsburger today embraces the brooding bitterness of Spalt with the spicy finish of Hallertau, though its European character is damaged more than most by U.S. serving temperatures. Try it at about 10°–15° C (46°–50° F). Notice, also, how the palate is enhanced by the relatively gentle carbonation. Augsburger (4.45% w; 5.5% v) has 80 percent malt and is lagered for six weeks. A similar but lower-priced beer is produced under the Regal Brau label. Huber also brews a genuine Augsburger Dark, quite dry, fruity, and with a faint coffee aftertaste. A bock beer (4.6% w; 5.75% v) employing four different malts has been variously marketed under the Augsburger, Rhinelander, and Huber labels. The regular Huber and Rhinelander beers (both 3.6% w; 4.5% v) are clean-tasting, with some hop bitterness.

Augsburger*** Regal Brau*** Augsburger Dark** Bock*** Huber Rheinlander* ½

HUDEPOHL, *Cincinnati, Ohio*. A sizable (1 million barrels) independent brewery producing the Hudepohl, Hofbrau, and Burger brands, Hudepohl has a hoppy nose but a pronounced maltiness in the body and a slightly sweet aftertaste.

Hudepohl** Hofbrau* Burger*

LEINENKUGEL, *Chippewa Falls, Wisconsin.* This is becoming something of a cult brewery, although comparisons between little Leine and mighty Coors do no justice to either. Leinenkugel's (3.75% w; 4.6% v) has a light, smooth palate, with a more substantial body than Coors, probably deriving from the use of six-row barley. Whole Clusters are used, and the beer has quite a lot of hop bouquet. The brewery also has the lighter Chippewa Pride and Bosch beers (both 3.5% w; 4.37% v). An excellent Bock is produced, malty without being sweet (5.0% w; 6.25% v). Leinenkugel is around the corner from the Falls, and both the brewery and the town get their water from the Big Eddy spring.

Leinenkugel's** Chippewa Pride* Bock***

MILLER, *Milwaukee, Wisconsin.* The second largest company in the U.S., owned by Philip Morris. Miller's genius lies in marketing. It popularized light beers, a reflection also of its technological dexterity, and perhaps the most agreeable of its products is the once-famous and now-neglected Miller High Life. Its U.S.–produced rendition of the German Löwenbräu has done little to enhance the credibility of such licensing arrangements.

Miller High Life*

PABST, *Milwaukee, Wisconsin.* Another giant, though a far lesser one in volume and relatively conservative in its policies. Pabst's principal brand, Blue Ribbon (3.75% w; 4.6% v), has a chewy character deriving from the house yeast. The company has a lower-priced beer called Red, White, and Blue, and a super-premium called Andeker (3.9% w; 4.8% v), long ago inspired by the Bavarian brewing abbey of Andechs. In recent years, Pabst's Andeker, an all-malt beer, has taken on the decisive firmness of two-row barley and the assertiveness and aroma of Styrian hops. The company should be a little less grudging in the distribution of this well-made beer.

Blue Ribbon*½ Red, White and Blue* Andeker***

PICKETT, *Dubuque, Iowa.* The movie-makers' favourite brewery, and one that deserves more support from its own community. Pickett's was a location in the film "F.I.S.T." and was featured under its own name in "Take This Job and Shove It", the story of the takeover of an independent brewery by a conglomerate. Pickett's own future has been in the balance on more than one occasion. It was at the point of closure as the Dubuque Star brewery when it was acquired, at the beginning of the 1970s, by Joe Pickett, who had recently retired after a lifetime as a brewmaster with a dozen or more companies. With his wife and sons, he has run the brewery ever since, although financial control is in the hands of the Midwestern farmers' co-operative, Agri Industries.

The name Dubuque Star, and the old Edelweiss brand from Chicago, are still used for dry, fruity, slightly sharp and quenching beers (both 3.9% w; 4.8% v). At a similar strength, a premium beer called, simply, Pickett's brewed from two-row barley and with the use of some imported Hallertaus. This 75 percent malt beer has a lighter body and more hop character. The brewery also has several minor brands. Pickett's has its own well, the original copper kettle, some wooden tanks, and interesting steam machinery. The brewery stands on the banks of the Mississippi, with a steamboat moored nearby, and welcomes visitors.

Dubuque Star* ½ Edelweiss* ½ Pickett's**

POINT, *Stevens Point, Wisconsin.* The top U.S. beer in a celebrated tasting carried out by Chicago columnist Mike Royko in 1973 was Point Special, the only year-round brand from this little family brewery. "The old saying when you're out of Point, you're out of town' is no longer applicable in the light of this worldwide recognition", suggests a somewhat extravagant citation from the Wisconsin legislature, signed by the Speaker of the Assembly and the President of the Senate and displayed in the brewery's reception room.

Point Special (3.7% w; 4.6% v) is a fairly full-bodied, well-balanced beer. It is brewed in a pre-Prohibition copper kettle, and starts its fermentation in a wooden tank. Wooden lagering tanks are also used. Point also has a well-made Bock, available only in February and March (4.2% w; 5.25% v).

Point Special** Point Bock***

SCHELL, *New Ulm, Minnesota.* A wine-like taste and aroma was detected in Schell's basic beer by U.S. writer James Robertson. He was probably tasting the esters in this fruity brew, which has very much the character of Schell's hard well-water and of six-row barley. The brewery also has a light-bodied super-premium called Ulmer, with 80 percent malt, as well as fairly light beers under the Steinhaus and Fitger labels and a hoppier brew called Export, produced allegedly according to an old recipe (all about 3.5% w; 4.3% v).

Schell's* Ulmer* ½

SCHLITZ, *Milwaukee, Wisconsin.* In the days when it was making Milwaukee famous, Schlitz was the biggest brewing company in the U.S.. Its decline makes a cautionary tale for brewers everywhere. Schlitz started cutting corners in production in the early 1970s, and its sales slipped. In the league of major brewers, it fell to third place, then fourth, with the fifth- and sixth-ranking brewers threatening to overtake. In recent years, Schlitz has leaned over backwards to improve the quality of its products, but there has not been a commensurate restoration of sales. It is easier to lose a good reputation than to regain one. It is also true that, while quality has improved, Schlitz beers still lack personality. Schlitz itself is a rather light beer, with a faintly geranial hop character. Even the super-premium Erlanger, a quality product brewed wholly with barley malt, is disappointingly unmemorable. Erlanger is a revival of an old U.S. brand name, originally inspired by the brewing town in Bavaria.

Schlitz* Erlanger**

SCHOENLING, *Cincinnati, Ohio.* The smaller of the two independent brewers in Cincinnati, and notable for its Little Kings Cream Ale. This diffident U.S. style is not normally found in the Midwest, and is perhaps evidence of Cincinnati's eastern flavour. Little Kings is full-bodied, fluffy, a little carbonic perhaps, but a good example of the style.

Little Kings Cream Ale**

STROH'S, *Detroit, Michigan.* Gaining popularity with more aggressive marketing, especially since it spread its wings through the purchase of Schaefer. Stroh's is very proud of its use of fire-brewing—using a direct flame, instead of steam, to heat the kettles, thus producing a good rolling boil that is held to improve the fullness and smoothness of flavour. The method was abandoned at one stage but was reintroduced in 1912 after a member of the Stroh family became convinced of its superiority while on a brewery-visiting trip in Europe. Until recently, Stroh's claimed to be the only U.S. brewery using direct fire, but the technique is now employed by several boutique breweries. The principal product, Stroh's Bohemian, has a hoppy nose but some maltiness in its fairly light body. The brewery has a lighter brand called Goebel, and a rather sweet Bock.

Stroh's Bohemian*½ Goebel* Bock*½

WALTER, *Eau Claire, Wisconsin.* At the end of a quiet elm-lined street in a town of white-painted clapboard houses, Walter's is a family brewery and very much a part of the community. In a copper kettle dating from 1889, and with the use of whole Yakima hops and some fairly respectable lagering times, two principal beers are made. The hoppy Walter's Special (about 3.9% w; 4.8% v) with 65 percent malt, is the more interesting of the two. This product was originally brewed as a Christmas special. The regular Walter's (about 3.6% w; 4.5% v) is very dry, clean, and rather light. The brewery tries to distinguish its low-calorie beer from the rest by describing it, quite misleadingly, as a light ale. It is nothing of the sort. Walter's has several other minor brands.

Walter's Special*½ Walter's *½

THE EAST

The natives seem hardly to notice, and it isn't immediately evident to the visitor, but the East remains even
today an ale-producing region on a significant scale. In
so doing, it reveals its British heritage, if somewhat
vestigially. Perhaps the ales of the East live such a quiet
life because they are so typical of the U.S. brews in their
pallor and palate. It is a paradox that the Eastern ale-
brewers, while proudly upholding the tradition of top-
fermentation, have assimilated stylistically while ale
fundamentalism has been introduced by the upstart
revivalists of the West.

It says a great deal about Eastern attitudes that New
York City has in recent years let both of its local
breweries fall to other states. Rheingold moved to New
Jersey, then closed, and the product is now brewed by
Schmidt's of Philadelphia. Schaefer, having taken over
Piels, moved to Pennsylvania. Schaefer is still extant, but
under the ownership of Stroh's, the Detroit brewery.
Although Schaefer has lost its independence, it remains
very much an Eastern name, and that is true of all eight
Pennsylvania breweries. Each is either regional or truly
local. In that respect, Pennsylvania, with its blending of
British and German traditions, survives as one of the
most important brewing states.

BALLANTINE, *Cranston, Rhode Island.* The most famous ales in
the U.S. no longer give their name to the brewery where
they were produced, but they should. The various
Ballantine ales moved to the Narragansett brewery in
Cranston, one of several belonging to Falstaff, a company
not otherwise noted for specialty beers. Falstaff bought
and closed the Ballantine plant in Newark, New Jersey, in
1972.

Ballantine ales have always been East Coast favourites,
but they have been rather peripatetic; they began their life
in the ale-brewing city of Albany, New York, having been
fathered by Peter Ballantine, an immigrant from Ayr,
Scotland. (He appears not to have been related to the
whisky Ballantines, although their firm was established at
about the same time.) There remains in private circula-
tion a number of bottles of the renowned Ballantine's
Burton Ale, now twenty or thirty years old. This remarkable ale was aged for up to ten years in tanks that were
gradually tapped and replenished, like the sherry *solera*.
At the time, the brewery produced its own hop oils by a
method of steam distillation similar to that employed to
make *grappa*. Burton had a proud 60 units of bitterness,
compared to 12 to 24 in regular U.S. beers.

Burton is no longer produced by Ballantine, but its
equally legendary IPA (India Pale Ale, another British
designation) survives. Like a half-forgotten celebrity,
thought by some admirers to have retired and by others
to be dead, Ballantine's has been living in quiet obscurity

in Rhode Island. Now, it is making something of a comeback. Because it is, in the U.S. context, such an unusual product, IPA merits close attention. It is brewed from a high density (19° Plato, 1076 British) with Brewer's Gold and Yakima in the kettle, fermented for two weeks, dry hopped, and aged in wood for four to five months. It was a stroke of luck that Narrangansett already had wooden tanks. IPA's colour is a rich copper in the British tradition, its head thick and rocky, its nose and palate intensely aromatic (45 units of bitterness), and its body firm and full (6.0% w; 7.5% v). In 1980, Ballantine added another ale to its range by reintroducing Brewer's Gold (5.7% w; 7.1% v), a product named after its principal hop although the epithet also describes its colour. This varietal ale made its return with 30 units of bitterness and, appropriately, with the characteristically sweet bouquet of Brewer's Gold hops. The same bouquet characterizes the basic Ballantine Ale (4.5% w; 5.6% v) also golden in colour and with 23 units of bitterness. Since the regular product is much less memorable than its bigger brothers, it is as well to remember that more than one type of ale is produced by Ballantine. The brewery also has a moderately interesting Porter, under the Narrangansett label, and some rather ordinary lager beers.

IPA**** Brewer's Gold*** Ballantine Ale**½
Narrangansett Porter***½

CHAMPALE, *Trenton, New Jersey.* The brewery's main product is a curiosity, and an engaging one. The product known as Champale (5.5% w; 6.8% v) is an "extra dry" malt liquor that also comes in fruit flavors: citrus and grenadine. It is said that in the past, grenadine was added to malt liquor in bars in much the way that peach essence was mixed with bourbon in the cocktails that were the predecessors of Southern Comfort. In Europe, the Belgians sometimes add grenadine to beer and the Germans their dash of raspberry or woodruff to Berliner weisse, while in Britain, lager-and-lime is an occasional summer drink. There is thus some antecedence to what seems otherwise a wholly gimcrack proposition. Champagne it isn't; nor is it in any way a serious beer to compare with the pink framboise or cherry kriek of Belgium.

FRED KOCH, *Dunkirk, New York.* Some interesting new products are in gestation at this small brewery in upstate ale country as a result of its takeover by the British company Vaux in 1981. In Britain, Vaux is a middle-sized brewing group, decidedly regional, with its markets concentrated in Northern England and Scotland. Unable to grow easily in Britain because of the tied-house system, it has expanded by a series of modest acquisitions. Fred Koch is best known for its Black Horse Ale, a strangely ubiquitous brew. Black Horse was originally a Canadian ale, produced by Dow and distributed in the U.S. by Fred Koch. When Dow was swallowed by Carling, production of the brand for the U.S. market was taken over by Koch. In order to ensure a wider distribution, arrangements were also made with the Champale breweries in New Jersey and Virginia to produce Black Horse Ale. Now that the little Koch brewery has the backing of Vaux, there is no doubt it will make more aggressive efforts to promote Black Horse as its own product. Black Horse is produced by bottom-fermentation, but is otherwise reminiscent of the Canadian ales.

Black Horse Ale* ½

GENESEE, *Rochester, New York.* The biggest producer of cream ale, which accounts for 40 percent of the output of this fast-growing brewery. If anyone knows exactly what the term cream ale means, and that is an open question, presumably it must be Genesee. The company is noticeably secretive, but the fact is that its cream ale is made by the blending of a small proportion of top-fermented brew with a lager quantity of a bottom-fermented lager beer. The end result has some ale character in its slight fruitiness, but is very reticent and smooth. Genesee Cream Ale (3.8% w; 4.75% v) has a pale, golden colour.

The company also has a conventional top-fermented ale called 12-Horse (4.0% w; 5.0% v) also golden in colour, with a more estery character and a fuller body. Neither is especially well-hopped, and this mildness is very much a house characteristic of Genesee products. In recent years, 12-Horse has come to be regarded as the brewery's premium product, taking over this role from a lager beer called Fyfe and Drum that has been phased out. The company also has a regular bottom-fermented lager known simply as Genesee Beer, which is notably full-bodied and smooth. Genesee is one of the very few breweries that still has its own maltings, some miles away at Sodus Point, on Lake Ontario. It is a situation that can only enhance the products.

Genesee Cream Ale** ½ 12-Horse Ale*** Genesee Beer* ½

IRON CITY, *Pittsburgh, Pennsylvania.* The brand name is better known than the corporation, which is simply called the Pittsburgh Brewing Company. Iron City used to have some character, but in recent years the hopping rate has been reduced and the company's efforts have increasingly been put behind a light beer. Pittsburgh Brewing also produces a wide range of other brands for the amusement of can collectors.

Iron City*

JONES, *Smithton, Pennsylvania.* Best known by its brand name, Stoney's. A small brewery with a capacity of 170,000 barrels, producing characterful beers for a loyal local audience in the shadow of Pittsburgh.

Stoney's*

LION, *Wilkes-Barre, Pennsylvania.* Once known among devotees for its licorice-tasting Stegmaier Porter, but these days heavily committed to supermarket and generic brands. Its own labels includes Gibbons, Liebotschaner, and Bartels.

F.X. MATT, *Utica, New York.* Francis Xavier Matt still runs this pretty, friendly brewery founded by his grandfather in 1888, and uses the brand-name Utica Club after its home town. The brewery is well-regarded for its Utica Club Cream Ale, made wholly by top-fermentation, without any blending; its top-and-bottom blended Fort Schuyler Beer; and its well-attenuated malt liquor called Maximus Super (5.2% w; 6.5% v). This is an interesting beer of good quality, with a hoppy nose and some estery sweetness in the palate. There is also a Utica Club Pilsener, and a more full-bodied and lightly hopped lager called Matt's Premium, which gains some fruitiness from fermentation at slightly higher temperatures than those normally used. The brewery uses rice as an adjunct, employs a Canadian ale yeast and its own lager culture, pursues maturation periods of four to five weeks for its premium products, krausens, and favours isinglass finings.

Cream Ale**½ Fort Schuyler**½ Maximus Super***
Pilsener* Matt's Premium**

ROLLING ROCK, *Latrobe, Pennsylvania.* As something of a cult brand, Rolling Rock is better known than the company that produces it, the Latrobe Brewing Company. Perhaps Rolling Rock's place in the beer-drinker's consciousness owes a little to the company's single-mindedness in concentrating on only one brand. Latrobe shows equal singularity in the manner in which it equips and maintains its superb brewery. Rolling Rock is a very well-made beer, with a pronounced hop character and a body that is malty but lightened by the use of rice as an adjunct. It is crystal clean, but rather weak in its finish.

Rolling Rock**½

SCHMIDT, *Philadelphia, Pennsylvania.* With hall upon hall of magnificent wooden fermenting and lagering vessels, constantly maintained with straw and linseed oil, and all still in use to augment more conventional equipment, Schmidt's is one of the most impressive independent breweries. It is also one of the bigger independents, with a capacity of 3.5 million barrels. The regular Schmidt's beer, fairly full-bodied and slightly estery, has more character than many U.S. lagers, but the company also produces a wide range of other interesting products. The most noteworthy among these is the only Czechoslovakian-style dark beer to be produced in the U.S.. By now, its lineage has been stretched somewhat, but Prior Double Dark (4.0% w; 5.0% v) was originally a Czech product, brewed by agreement in the U.S. by a company, in Norristown, Pennsylvania, that was acquired by Schmidt. Although the term Double has no particular significance, Prior is distinctive in that it contrives to be full-bodied without being heavy, malty without being sweet, and indeed to have a characteristically Czechoslovakian dryness in its hoppy finish. The hops used are not Czechoslovakian, but American Cascades are employed, and their geranial quality probably has something to do with the distinctive finish. A fairly high hopping rate helps contribute to about 25 units of bitterness and is used to balance the sweetness of the caramel malts. Lagering takes at least four weeks, and sometimes more than six. Some nonsensical advertising claims have been made for Double Dark, including the suggestion that it is America's only world-class beer. That soubriquet belongs to Anchor Steam, but Prior is the most distinctive dark beer produced in the U.S..

Schmidt's also produces a top-fermenting ale called Tiger Head (3.75% w; 4.6% v), golden in colour, that derives a lot of character from its yeast but, although hopped twice in the kettle, is fairly mild nonetheless. The brewery also now makes the famous McSorley's ale (3.8% w; 4.75% v), which originated in the bar of the same name in East 7th Street, New York City, and which over the years has been produced in several different places. McSorley's came to the brewery as a bottom-fermenting product, and remains such. However, recent brewers of McSorley's have gone to some pains to ensure that it is endowed with some character and Schmidt's, too, is taking this approach. Imported Hallertaus are used in the kettle, the beer is dry-hopped, and the brewery's own hop oils are also used to impart additional bouquet. McSorley's has 30 units of bitterness, and a golden colour.

Schmidt's*½ Prior Double Dark**** Tiger Head**½ McSorley's*** Ortlieb*½ Rheingold*½

STRAUB, *St. Mary's, Pennsylvania.* A charming, tiny (40,000 barrels) local brewery producing just one brand. Straub Beer has a hoppy bouquet and a fairly light body, with a very dry palate and a full, rather grainy aftertaste. The brewery boasts that it does not use corn syrups, although flake corn is employed. No additives are used, and the beer is very thoroughly matured.

Straub Beer**

YUENGLING, *Pottsville, Pennsylvania.* The oldest operating brewery in the U.S., founded in 1829, and known especially for what it grandly describes as "The Celebrated" Pottsville Porter (4.0% w; 5.0% v). This is brewed with dark malt specially roasted for Yuengling. It has a good roasty character and is quite dry, with a good head and a soft but rather light body. For the style, it is relatively low on hop character. At a similar strength, Yuengling produces the dry-hopped U.S.-style Chesterfield Ale. This is a clean, dry, floral beer with an agreeably rounded finish. Both were for many years top-fermented but they are now made by the lager method. Yuengling also has a Pilsener-type beer and one or two other rather mild conventional lagers.

Pottsville Porter*** Chesterfield Ale** ½ Yuengling Pilsner**

NEWMAN'S *Albany, New York.* When it went into business right at the end of 1981, the William S. Newman brewery made history by reintroducing to the New World the tradition of naturally conditioned draught ale. The brewery's principal product is a hoppy Pale Ale inspired by the draught bitter at the Ringwood brewery in England, a well-respected boutique where Bill Newman learned his craft. Newman, an American, also has a strong, dark brown ale (5.8%w; 7.25%v) called Winter Warmer. Each is available only on draught and in a very local distribution area. It is too early to assess these products, and it remains to be seen whether American bar-owners can adapt to the keeping and serving of a product as temperamental as naturally conditioned draught. Nor is it certain that such an individualistic product will find a market in the U.S., though there are many enthusiasts who will support it. If Newman succeeds in his heroic venture, he will undoubtedly inspire many others. He will also have brought back to Albany some of the distinction it once enjoyed as a center of ale-brewing.

THE SOUTH

For the drinker in search of distinctive beer styles, the South has little to offer. Without the old big cities of the East and Midwest, it has not had the size or style of communities that support traditional specialty beers. Without quite the inclinations or aspirations of the West, it has yet to see boutique breweries, or even a really broad selection of imports, although both phenomena may well be on their way. The climate encourages beer-drinking, but it does not favour what Southerners might term sippin' beers. Nor has the restrictive influence of the Bible Belt helped the development of discriminating palates in the matter of drink. There is much local pride in the two Texan breweries, Lone Star and Pearl, but that is a matter of chauvinism rather than any more complex criteria.

DIXIE, *New Orleans, Louisiana.* Well-known small (300,000 barrel) independent that survived when the local Jax brewery ceased operations. Skillful marketing has helped Dixie to stay in business, producing light, fruity, and quite characterful beers.

Dixie Beer* ½

DUNCAN, *Auburndale, Florida.* Lots of supermarket brands are produced at this small brewery recently acquired by Heileman of Wisconsin (see p. 114).

LONE STAR, *San Antonio, Texas.* Its beer, of the same name, is yeasty, with a good head, hoppy nose, dry palate, excellent bead, and some estery fruitiness in the aftertaste. Lone Star is owned by Olympia, of Washington State (see p. 110).

Lone Star**

PEARL, *San Antonio, Texas.* Under its own name, a producer of light, malty beers. Pearl also produces Jax beer. The company is now under the same control as Falstaff.

Pearl* Jax*

SPOETZL, *Shiner, Texas.* Famous for its Bavarian-style, dark, full-bodied beer in its days under the stewardship of brewmaster Kosmas Spoetzl. This tradition persisted for a time after the death of Spoetzl and during the reign of his daughter, "Miss Celie", but endures no longer. The small (60,000 barrel) brewery is still locally owned, but produces very ordinary beers. The brewery's colourful architectural style, reminiscent of a border fort, is poor consolation for the loss of a distinctive beer, although the company's survival is in itself a cause for thanks.

Shiner Premium*

LATIN AMERICA

The Caribbean

There are two points of stylistic significance in the beers
of the Caribbean. Although neither is of major importance, both endow the region with some interest for the
beer-drinker. One is a tradition of stouts that dates back
at least to the early 1800s, when Guinness had a special
export product, remembered as being of high quality
and lively hop character, called West Indies Porter.
Today, there are local Guinness breweries producing
the splendid Foreign Extra Stout in Jamaica and Trinidad, while sweeter palates are served by Mackeson and
one or two local brands. Stouts are thought to be
energizers, if not aphrodisiacs, and similar properties
are attributed to the malt-extract products popular in
the region. The other tradition, dating back only to the
middle of the 20th century, is the production of lagers
that are notably clean-tasting as a consequence of very
light hopping and thorough attenuation. The classic
examples are Red Stripe, of Jamaica, and Banks, of
Barbados, to which might be added Carib, of Trinidad,
which is less well-known outside the West Indies. The
object of the high attenuation is to get as much alcohol
content as possible out of a conventional gravity; being
spirit-drinkers, the people of the rum countries like
some potency even in their beer. The purpose of the
low hopping is to mitigate any dryness caused by the
degree of attenuation; with its hot climate, the Caribbean beers must be quenching. Most of the Caribbean
nations have breweries, either locally owned or as
associates of European majors, notably Heineken.

Latin America

Mexico is by far the most interesting brewing nation in
Latin America, and its products deserve more respect
than they get. Their reputation is growing with their
increasing availability in the U.S., but their acceptance
there is still tinged with a patronizing ethnic chauvinism among non-Hispanic drinkers. What is not understood is that Mexico has a specifically Viennese brewing

tradition, dating from the time when the country was an outpost of the Hapsburg empire. This interesting antecedence is revealed by products like the Viennese-style amber Dos Equis and Indio Oscura, and the darker Leon Negra and Noche Buena. Regrettably, the Mexican brewers themselves fail to proclaim the nature of their products, often preferring to promote their beers in the fatuous and sexist macho manner that is thought by some to be appropriate for the U.S. market. If this is how the producers see their products, then the future integrity of Mexican beers must be in some doubt. That is a shame: although none of the beers is by any means a world classic, some are distinctive and interesting by the standards of brewing in the Americas as a whole.

Quality and character aside, Mexico is one of the world's major brewing nations in terms of volume (with Brazil level-pegging). All of the Latin American countries have brewing industries, and names like Brahma (of Brazil) and Callao (of Peru) occasionally find their way to other parts of the world. German immigration to various South American countries has influenced brewing, and most of the beers are relatively full-bodied lagers, though stouts can be found occasionally.

AUSTRALASIA

It has been bruited about in recent years that Australia produces some fearsomely good beers. Most of the bruiting has been done by Australians, rucksacking their way through London and New York. In considering these claims, it has to be appreciated that Australians are very chauvinistic people, the inhabitants of one state being reluctant to drink the beers of another, let alone to concede that anything British or American might be potable. It has also to be realized that Australians drink their beers so cold as to anaesthetize the palate, thus rendering imperceptible any differences between one brand and another. Nor are there enormous distinctions in character among the principal brands. Most Australian beers are pale lagers, and it is in their national character to be full-bodied, but sweetish rather than malty. Most have an alcohol content of around 3.9 percent by weight, 4.8 by volume. None is outstanding, although one or two are very drinkable. The most interesting beers, the handful of ales and stouts, are often the least appreciated by Australians. Although things may be changing, this is especially true of Cooper's Sparkling Ale, the most interesting beer in Australasia.

What it lacks in refinement, Australia makes up for in enthusiasm, and it is one of the world's biggest beer-drinking nations in terms of consumption per head. In recent years, New Zealand has fallen behind in this respect. Like Australia, it has the odd interesting beer, but New Zealand's everyday brews are bland. Though both countries are large in land area, they are small in population and support only a few brewery companies. New Zealand has only three. Australia, after a spate of mergers and takeovers, is now down to six, which does not augur well for some of its funkier little beers.

CARLTON AND UNITED, *Melbourne.* Traditionally, this is the giant of the Australian brewing industry, although it is being challenged by mergers among its rivals. The basic Carlton Draught is a bit stronger than average, with a slightly fuller colour than its contemporaries but with a rather neutral character. Carlton Crown Lager is pale, full, and sweetish. So is Foster's, just another of the company's brands in Australia although it has become an Antipodean legend elsewhere in the world. Melbourne Bitter and Victoria Bitter are both lagers, the former fairly dry and the latter rather light in character. A product called Malt Ale is also a lager, appropriately full in flavour and body. There is also an evenly balanced Abbots Lager.

Carlton Draught**½ Crown Lager* Foster's*½
Melbourne Bitter** Victoria Bitter* Malt Ale**
Abbots Lager*½

CASCADE, *Tasmania.* Hops and malt are both major crops in Tasmania. The Cascade brewery produces clean-tasting beers with a characteristic pale amber colour. Its Red and Blue Label brands are dry, and its Green Label is slightly stronger and more bitter. Cascade also has a malty Stout (5.6% w; 7.0% v). The company also owns Boag's beers.

Red Label**½ Blue Label**½ Green*** Stout***

CASTLEMAINE TOOHEYS, *Brisbane, Sydney.* Castlemaine produces perhaps the best of Australia's everyday lagers, a malty, rounder beer called XXXX (ordered phonetically as Four-ex). The company has something of a tradition of folksy brand names, as evidenced by the various stouts it has made over the years. In 1980, Castlemaine, of Brisbane, was in a merger with Toohey's, of Sydney, historically the favoured brewery of that city's Catholic community. Toohey's produces a range of typically sweet Australian beers, and a well-attenuated but fruity Old. The epithet old is applied to beers of the dark ale type, a reminder of British traditions that predate the introduction of lager-brewing to Australia in the 1880s. Toohey's Old also appears as Hunters Ale at the group's brewery in Newcastle, New South Wales. A small share in Castlemaine Tooheys is held by the British group Allied Breweries.

Castlemaine XXXX**½ Toohey's Old, Hunter Ale***

COOPER, *Adelaide.* This brewery's extraordinary Cooper's Sparkling Ale is one of the world's most distinctive beers. In some markets, the term sparkling has been removed by legislators too pedantic to appreciate irony. In order to see how such an effusively cloudy beverage could ever have been described as being sparkling, it is necessary to recall that it was introduced at a time when a great many beers were opaque. In its isolation, produced by a brewery seemingly still existing in the Colonial era,

Cooper's Sparkling Ale may well be the nearest surviving beer to the type of pale ale produced in England during the late 18th century. Recently, it temporarily lost its characteristic copper colour, but the brewery says that was simply the function of that season's malt. The notion that there might be only certain vintage years for Cooper's is delightful, but it would be better were the brewery to ensure a supply of suitable malt, since the kilning is also a part of the character. Cooper's (4.25% w; 5.3% v) is fermented in wooden casks, and conditioned in the bottle—hence its yeasty sediment. A lower-gravity Dinner Ale (3.8% w; 4.75% v) is produced by the same method. Cooper's also has an excellent, robust, bottle-conditioned Extra Stout (5.5% w; 6.9% v). The company also produces a colourful range of lager beers.

Cooper's Sparkling Ale***** Dinner Ale**** Extra Stout**** ½

DOMINION, *Auckland, New Zealand*. The dubious distinction of having invented the continuous-fermentation process is accorded to this company. Dominion Bitter is its principal product.

Dominion Bitter*

LEOPARD, *Hastings, New Zealand*. By far the smallest of the three brewing companies in New Zealand, and jointly controlled by Heineken and Malayan Breweries. Its basic Leopard beer is light and pleasant but undistinguished.

Leopard Beer**

NEW ZEALAND BREWERIES, *Wellington*. This brewing concern is known in some export markets for its assertively hoppy and crisp pilsener-style Steinlager (about 4.0% w; 5.0% v). At home, the company produces a range of beers under the Lion name, which have more colour but less character.

Steinlager***

SOUTH AUSTRALIAN BREWING, *Adelaide*. This lager brewery produces sweetish beers under the West End label and drier products with the brand name Southwark. South Australian has a 25 percent share in its neighbor Cooper's, which is a public company, although still controlled by the founding family. A 20 percent share in South Australian (and in Cascade) is held by Carlton and United.

West End Bitter* Southwark Bitter**

SWAN, *Perth*. A well-known western brewery, Swan produces sweetish beers under its own name, and drier ones with the Emu label. Swan also owns Hannan's of Kalgoorlie.

Swan Lager* Emu Lager* ½

TOOTH, *Sydney.* The beers brewed by Tooth are traditionally the Protestant counterblast to Toohey's Catholic beers in the Sydney market. The firm's founder, John Tooth, came from the hop-growing English county of Kent in the 1830s. In 1981, control of the brewery was taken over by an Australian shipping company. Tooth's is especially well-known for its excellent, dryish Sheath Stout (3.9% w; 4.9% v), an outstanding example of the style. It also has a well-liked old (called XXX), and its flagship lager is its KB (Kent Brewery). This carries the German-sounding Resch's label, which was acquired in 1929. There are several other interesting products, although it remains to be seen whether the traditionalist attitudes of the company will survive under its new ownership. Not long before it was itself taken over, Tooth acquired the Courage brewery in Melbourne, the product of an unsuccessful venture into the Australian market by the British company.

Sheaf Stout**** ½ Tooth's Old*** ½ KB* ½

ASIA & AFRICA

Asia

Westerners no longer express surprise that Japan enjoys success in the production of other artefacts of European and American life, but the notion of mighty breweries under the eastern sun still causes raised eyebrows. It shouldn't. British colonial activities in the Indian sub-continent, German influence in pre-revolutionary China, and the U.S. "opening up" of Japan in the 1850s all paved the way for the introduction of beer-brewing to the East. Local conditions, although they are significant, are not as critical to the success of brewing as they are to the making of wine or whisky, and it is true in any case that the most northerly parts of China and Japan are on latitudes similar to those of Wisconsin and Bavaria. The Tsingtao brewery, in northern China, is especially proud of its locally grown hops, and the Japanese also grow substantial amounts of malting barley, though they augment their own output with imports from Denmark, Czechoslovakia, and elsewhere.

In much the way that Chinese food is said to be only temporarily satisfying, Western legend has it that Asian beers are made from rice. This is less than wholly true. Even in the West, rice is sometimes used in brewing as an adjunct to malted barley. The best-known case is that of the world's biggest-selling beer, Budweiser, the product of 70 percent barley malt, with rice as an adjunct. Similar proportions of rice are used by some, though by no means all, Eastern brewers, but a higher percentage would pose fermentation problems.

Japan is, in volume although not in stylistic influence, among the world's leading brewing nations. Consumption of beer per head in Japan is modest, but it is growing, and the country does have a large population. Japanese brewers also export extensively in Asia and to some U.S. cities. This volume of production is in the hands of only five brewing companies, among which Kirin is the largest anywhere in the world outside the U.S. Two other internationally known lagers, Tiger Beer and San Miguel, originate from Singapore/Malaysia and from The Philippines, respectively, Thailand has beers that are respected beyond her borders, Sri Lanka has top-fermenting ales and stouts, and almost every Asian country except those most rigidly Muslim has at least one brewery.

CHINA

The fashionability of Tsingtao beer in New York arose originally from its availability in some Chinatown restaurants. It can occasionally be found in London's Chinatown, too, although erratically. The beer is brewed from supposedly "sweet" spring water issuing from granite in the richly fertile mountain foothills near the resort of Tsingtao in the province of Shantung. In its architecture and atmosphere, the region still evokes its 19th-century period under German influence. The brewery was founded by Germans, and was then in Japanese hands for a time. but is now proudly Chinese. The basic Tsingtao is a dry pilsener-style beer with a good hop character, although its overall quality seems to vary, suggesting an inconsistent supply of good malting barley. It is a shame that Tsingtao Porter, and the beers of the many other Chinese breweries, are not more widely available in the West. Among those that are to be found, a brand called Snowflake is quite impressive, Shanghai less so.

JAPAN

As a response to the lightness, delicacy, and freshness of Japanese food, the country's brewers have sought a similar character in their beers. The principal products are lagers that are light in body and very delicate in their hop character. They usually have an alcohol content of around 3.6 percent by weight, 4.5 by volume, although there are stronger premium products, and Black beers that are broadly in the münchner style, although with a slightly higher alcohol content (about 4.0% w; 5.0% v). Medium and sweet stouts are also produced. Kirin's basic lager is the least light-tasting of the Japanese beers, with a rather malty, sticky body. The company has a relatively strong premium called Meinbräu (5.2% w; 6.4% v). Sapporo has a hoppier basic lager and at about the same strength, an all-malt premium beer called Yebisu. Asahi's beers seem to be the least consistent of the Japanese products, and are given to some acidic fruitiness. Suntory, the company that pioneered the production of unpasteurized beers in Japan by the use of very fine filtration, has the lightest and cleanest-tasting of the basic lagers. It also has a premium beer rather misleading called Märzen (4.0% w; 5.0% v), all-malt, Saaz-hopped, and lagered for two months rather than the usual four weeks.

THE PHILIPPINES

"The best beer in the world" is San Miguel, of the Philippines, according to a U.S. banker polled on the topic by *Business Week* magazine. Such an unqualified response calls into question the alleged caution of the men who manage our money, but it is some indication of the way in which San Miguel has established its name, not only in Asia but also in the U.S. market. Most San Miguel beer sold in the U.S. comes from the parent company in The Philippines, though some originates from the branch breweries in Spain. Whichever the source, the Hispanic brand-name, deriving from The Philippines' colonial past, is an advantage in markets like New York, Miami, and the Californian cities. San Miguel, in business since 1890, also has breweries in Hongkong, Indonesia and Papua New Guinea, and is a heavily diversified major trading company.

The popularity of the basic San Miguel lager in the U.S. is probably helped by its cleanness and lightness, since U.S. drinkers are accustomed to refreshing beers. It is, with about 20 units of bitterness, quite dry by U.S. standards; it has 80 per cent barley malt, and is lagered for three to four weeks (4.0% w; 5.0% v). San Miguel is in no way exceptional, but it is a well-made lager in the light, mild, international interpretation of the pilsener style. The company also has one of the better examples, outside Germany, of the dark münchner style (4.1% w; 5.1% v). This product emerged as the best dark lager in the 1980 International Beer Festival in San Francisco, though it has since then changed slightly in character, becoming less dry, roastier and richer. The Hongkong brewery also produces Sun Lik, (3.8% w; 4.75% v), a conventional lager. Despite its claim to use 80 percent barley malt and six weeks of lagering, this product has a disappointingly worthy character.

SINGAPORE/MALAYSIA

The trilogy *Time for Tiger* by Anthony Burgess took its title, with the brewery's permission, from a famous beer of the Far East. Tiger beer is brewed in Malaysia, where Burgess was living at the time, and in Singapore, with which city it is forever associated in the memories of Britain's armed forces. Although its renown rests primarily on evocation, and it is a perfectly ordinary pilsener-type lager, Tiger (4.0% w; 5.0% v) is nonetheless very drinkable. It has a good head, soft body, and delicately pleasing hop character, and in 1980 emerged at the top in a blindfold tasting of lagers carried out by the London *Sunday Times*. A slightly less hoppy lager of the same strength, called Anchor, is produced by the same company, Malayan Breweries, which was set up in 1929 by Heineken in association with a local soft-drinks firm, Fraser and Neave. The company also has a stout.

THAILAND

When the extraordinary subtlety of Thai food is taken into account, it is surprising that the country's two premium beers are actually quite assertive. Neither is widely available in the West, though they are often to be found in Thai restaurants. Thai Amarit is perhaps the hoppier, and Singha slightly fuller in palate (both about 3.8% w; 4.8% v).

AFRICA

The continent of Africa might, in a chauvinistic moment, claim to be the birthplace of beer, since it was the ancient Egyptians (along with the Babylonians, it must be admitted) who left the first, highly detailed accounts of brewing procedures. Like the Russians in the production of kvass, they used bread as a fermentable material. Today, millet, cassava, and palm sap are among the many local ingredients still used in the production of indigenous fermented drinks that are loosely described as beers. These African products survive as part of the regional culture, alongside the European brewing tradition implanted in different parts of the continent by the colonial powers during the late nineteenth century.

Although ale-brewing was introduced by the British in southern Africa, and still survives there vestigially, the stability and quenching quality of lagers found greater favour in the heat of the colonies. The Dutch in the south, and the Germans and Belgians in their colonies, all played a part in the spread of lager-brewing in Africa.

The British, through Allied Breweries, still have a stake in Tusker lager, in Kenya; the French are still active; so, most of all, are the Dutch, through Heineken, sometimes in partnership with Unilever or the Lambert bank in Belgium; even the Swiss have a few footholds. Many of these interests work in partnership with state-owned companies, producing local brands in countries all over the continent. One European company, headed by a member of the Haase family that once owned breweries in Breslau, Germany (now Wroclaw, Poland), exists purely for the purpose of this kind of co-operation. A particularly fine pilsener-type beer brewed with the help of Haase expertise can be found in Togo, but the great brewing nations of Africa are Nigeria and Zaire. Neither is important as a stylistic influence, but both are among the world's biggest beer-producers in terms of volume. South Africa, despite the dominance of a European colonial culture, is less important, though its Rupert/Rothman group has made its presence felt in the brewing industries of other countries like Denmark and Canada. The majority of African countries have breweries, though the resurgence of Islam has cast doubts over the future of some.

Index of Breweries and Brands

Abbaye de Bonne
  Esperance 65
Abbaye de Leffe
  Radieuse 59
Abbaye la Moinette 63
Abbot ale (Greene
  King) 78
Abbots lager 128
Abt (St. Sixtus) 57
Adelscott 92
Adnams 78
Aguila 100
Albani 49
Alfa 67
All Nations 84
Alpine Lager Beer 105
Altbier (D.A.B.) 34
Amstel 67
Anchor Steam 107
Anchor (Tiger) 133
Andechs 39-40
Andeker 115
Andreas Bock 40
Anheuser-Busch
  112-113
Animator 42
Arcen 67
Artois 59
Asahi 132
Astra 29, 30
Augsburger 114
Augustiner 40
Aventinus 45
Aying 40

Ballantine 118-119
Bank 125
Bank's 82
Bartel's 121
Bass 71, 73, 83
Bateman 79
Batham 82
Bavaria 67, 68
Bavaria St. Pauli 29, 110
Bayer (Bavarian) 49
Beamish 89
Beck's 30
Belhaven 86-87
Belle-vue 51
Benedict 60
Benskins 76
Bergbock Dunkel
  (Andechs) 40
Bergbock Hell
  (Andechs) 40
Best (Shep's) 77
Best (Timothy Taylor)
  81
Best Bitter (Courage)
  85
Best Bitter (Theakston)
  81
Bière Rousse (Pelforth)
  93
Bios 56
Bitter (Border) 86
Bitter (Brain) 86
Bitter (Eldridge Pope)
  85
Bitter (Felinfoel) 86
Bitter (Shep's) 77

Bitter (Thwaites) 82
Black Horse Ale 119-
  120
Blitz-Weinhard 108
Blue Label 101
Blue Label (Cascade)
  128
Blue Ribbon 115
Bock (Amstel) 67
Bock (Budel) 68
Bock (Felsenkeller)
  31-32
Bock (Huber) 114
Bock (Leinenkugel) 115
Bock (Pelforth) 93
Bock (Stroh's) 117
Boddingtons 79
Bok (Aass) 49
Bok (Grölsch) 68
Bokbier (Gulpen) 69
Boon 60
Border 85-86
Boulder Brewery 108
Boxer of Romanel-sur-
  Lausanne 95
Brador 105
Brain 86
Brakspear 75-76
Brand 68
Branik 25
Brasserie Nationale 65
Brau AG 96-97
Brew XI 84
Brewer's Choice 101
Brewer's Gold 119
Briljant 69
Brinckhoff's No. 1 36
Broadside 78
Broyhan Alt 33
Bruce's 76
Buckeye 103
Budel 68
Budvar 25
Budweiser (Anheuser-
  Busch) 113
Budweiser (Labatt) 104
Bulldog 85
Burger (Hudepohl) 114
Burt 78
Busch (Anheuser-
  Busch) 113

Cameron 79
Cantillon 60
Cardinal 95
Carib 125
Carl Funke Stern 35
Carling 103-104
Carlsberg 49-50
Carlton and United 128
Carnegie Porter 52
Cartwright 108-109
Cascade 128
Castelmaine Tooheys
  128
Caves Bruegel 61
CD Pils (Domestic) 40
CD Pils (Export) 40
Ceres 50
Champale 119
Cheshire English Pub
  Beer 80

Chess 52
Chesterfield Ale 123
Chevalier Marin 59
Chimay see Trappists
  of Chimay
Chippewa Pride 115
Chiswick Bitter 76
Christmas Ale (Anchor
  Steam) 107
Cisk 101
Classic (Dortmunder
  Kronen) 35
Club-Weisse (Spaten)
  46
Cold Spring 113
College Ale 74
Columbus 98
Cool Spring 104
Cooper 128-129
Coors 109
County 79
Courage 71, 74, 84-85
Cream Ale (F.X. Matt)
  121
Crown Lager 128
Crystal 104
Cuvée de l'Ermitage 65

D.A.B. (Dortmunder
  Actien Brewery) 34
Dalila 25
Danny Brown 82
Dark Lager
  (Holesovice) 27
Dart 52
De Bakker 110
De Keersmaeker 61
De Kluis 59-60
De Koninck 54
De Kroon 69
De Leeuw 69-70
De Neve 61
De Ridder 70
De Troch 61
Devenish 85
Devizes Pale Ale 85
Diekirch 65
Dinkelacker 40
Dinner Ale (Cooper's)
  129
Diplomat 26
Dixie 124
Dogbolter 76
Dominion 129
Dommels Pils 69
Donker (Old Brown) 70
Donnington 74
Doppelbock Dunkel
  (Andechs) 40
Doppelbock Hell
  (Andechs) 40
Dort (Gulpen) 69
Dortmunder Actien
  Brewery 34
Dortmunder (Bavaria) 68
Dortmunder Hansa 34
Dortmunder Kronen 35
Dortmunder Ritter 35
Dortmunder Stifts 35
Dortmunder Thier 35
Dortmunder Union
  Brauerei 36

Dos Equis 126
Double Dragon 86
Double Enghien 63
Double Maxim 82
Dow Porter 103
Drie Hoe4ijzers 70
Drybrough 87
Du Bocq/Brasserie
Centrale 63
D.U.B. (Dortmunder
Union Brauerei) 36
Dubbel (Trappists of
Westmalle) 57
Dubuque Star 116
Duivel 62
Duncan 124
Dunkel Export (Spaten)
45-46
Dunkel Spezial
(Riegele)
Dunkler Bock (Gösser)
97
Dunkler Bock
(Reininghaus) 98
Dupont 63
Duvel 55

Edel-Weizen 42
Edelweiss 116
Egill Skallagrimsson 52
80/-(Belhaven) 86-87
80/-Export (Maclay) 87
80/-(Lorimer) 87
Einbecker 30-31
E.K.U. (Erste
Kulmbacher Brewery)
41
Eldridge Pope 85
Elephant 50
Elgood 79
Emu Lager 129
Erlanger 117
Erste Kulmbacher
Brewery 41
ESB Extra Special
Bitter (Fuller) 76
Everards 83
Export (Aass) 49
Export Ale
(Moosehead) 105
Export Gold (Watney)
77
Export (Reininghaus)
98
Extra Dry (33) 94
Extra Special Bitter
(Fuller) 76
Extra Stout (Cooper's)
129
Extra Stout (Guinness)
90
Extra Stout (Labatt) 104
Eylenbosch 61

Faxe 50-51
Faxe Fad 51
Felinfoel 86
Felsenkeller 31-32
Ferdinand Schumacher
37
Festbock 97
Feuerfest 41

Fischer/Pêcheur 92
Fix 101
Floreffe 56
Foreign Extra Stout
(Guinness) 90
Fort Schuyler 121
Foster's 128
Fowler's 88
Fox DeLuxe 113
Frankenmuth Bavarian
113
Franziskus 45, 46
Fred Koch 119-120
Fremlins' Bitter 77
Friary Meux 76
Fuller 75, 76
Fürstenberg 41

Gale 76
Gambrinus 25-26
Gammel Porter 50
Gatzweiler 37
Gauloise 63
Gemeinde 113
Genesee 120
Geyer 113
Gibbons 121
Gibbs Mew 85
Ginder 59
Giraf 49
Girardin 61
Goebel 117
Goldbräu 98
Gold Keg 104
Gold Label (Carlsberg)
50
Gold Label (Whitbread)
77
Golden Mild (Timothy
Taylor) 81
Golden/Traditional
Scotch 87
Goose Eye 81
Gösser 96-97
Gouden Carolus 56
Grand Cru (De Kluis)
60
Green (Cascade) 128
Greenall Whitley 79-80
Greene King 78
Grenzquell 29, 30
Grimbergen 55
Grolsch 68
Guinness 89-90
Guinness (Labatt) 104
Gulpen 69

Hacker-Pschorr 41-42
Hall and Woodhouse 85
Hansa Brewery 34
Hartley's 80
Harvey 78
H.B. (Hofbräuhaus) 42
Hefe-Weissbier
(Paulaner) 44
Hefeweissbier (Spaten)
46
Hefeweizen (Riegele)
44
Heileman 114
Heineken 69
Heller Bock (Gösser) 97

Heller Bock
(Reininghaus) 98
Hengelo 69
Henninger 32
Henri Funck Battin 65
Henry Weinhard's
Private Reserve 108
Herforder 32
Herman Joseph's 109
Herrenhausen 32
Het Anker 56
Het Kapittel 57
Highgate mild 83-84
Higsons 80
Hoegaards Wit 60
Hofbräu (Hudepohl)
114
Hofbräuhaus (H.B.) 42
Holden 82
Holland Beer Extra
Stout 70
Holland Beer Pilsner
De Luxe 70
Holland Beer Special
70
Holsten 32-33
Holt 79
Hooijberg 69
Hook Norton 74
Hop Leaf 101
Huber 114
Hudepohl 114
Hungaria Lager 99
Hunter Ale 128
Hürlimann 95
Hydes 79

Im Füchschen 37
Imperator (Brand) 68
Imperial stout
(Carlsberg) 50
Ind Coope 76
India Pale Ale see IPA
Indio Oscura 126
Irish Ale Brewers 90
Irish Red Ale 109
Iron City 120
IPA (Ballantine) 118-
119
IPA (Eldridge Pope) 85
IPA (Labatt) 104
IPA(Wadworth) 85

Jax 124
Jenlain 92
Jennings 80
Jever Pilsener 29, 30
Jones 121
Jule (Aass) 47
Juløl 52
Jupiter 64

Kaiser Pilsner 32
Kaiserdom 42-43
Karlovac 101
KB (Kent Brewery) 130
Kegel Bräu 113
Keo 101
Ketje 59
Kindl 47
King and Barnes 78
Killian's 90

Kirin 131, 132
Kloster Andecher 39-40
Kloster Schwarz 43
Klosterbock Dunkel 43
Koff 51
Kronenbourg 93
Kronenpils 93
Kulmbacher Mönschof 43
Kulminator Dunkles Starkbier 41
Kulminator 28

Labatt 104
Lamot 64
Landlord 81
Latzenbier 37
Lees 79
Leinenkugel 115
Leon Negra 126
Leopard 129
Lett's Ruby Ale 90, 109
Liebotschaner 121
Liefmans 55
Lindeboom 70
Lindemans 61
Lidener-Gilde 33
Lion 121
Little Kings Cream Ale 117
Loburg 59
Local Bitter (Greenall Whitley) 80
Lolland-Falsters 51
London Bitter 77
London Pride 76
London Stout (Moosehead) 105
Lone Star 124
Lorimer 87
Löwenbräu 43
Lupo of Hochdorf 95
Lutèce 93

McEwan's and Younger's 87
McMullen 78
McSorley's 122
Macardle's 90
Mackeson 8, 77
Maclay 87
Maes 55
Magnus 67
Maibock (H.B.) 42
Maingold 43
Malayan Breweries 134
Malt Ale (Carlton and United) 128
Maltezer 70
Mann's Brown 77
Maredsous 55
Marston's 83
Martinsky Porter 26
Marzen (Gösser) 97
Matt, F.X. 121
Maximator 40
Maximus Super 121
Meinbräu (Kirin) 132
Meister Pils (D.A.B.) 34
Melbourne Bitter 128
Merrie Monk 83
Michalovce 26

Michelob 113
Mild (Felinfoel) 86
Miller 115
Mitchell and Butlers 83-84
Mitchells' 80
Molson 104-105
Moosehead 105
Moravia-Pils 33
Moretti 100
Morland's 74
Morrell's 74
Mort subite 61-62
Munchner Hell (Paulaner) 44
Munchner Hell (Spaten) 45-46
Murphy 90

Narragansett Porter 119
New Albion 110
New Zealand Breweries 129
Newcastle Breweries 80
Newman's 11, 123
Niksic 101
1900 63
Noche Buena 126
No. 3 (McEwan's/ Younger's) 87

Oerbier 56
O'Keefe Ale 103
Oktoberfest (Würzburger) 47
Old Alloa 87
Old Brewery Bitter 81
Old Dan 82
Old Peculier 81
Old Swan 84
Old Style (Heileman) 114
Old Timer 85
Old Vienna 103
Olde English 800 108
Olympia 110
Optimator (Spaten) 46
Oranjeboom 70
Orval 65
Oud Bruin (Amstel) 67
Oud Bruin (Bavaria) 68
Oud Bruin (Budel) 68
Oud Bruin (Grolsch) 68
Oud Bruin (Heineken) 69
Oud Limburgs 67
Oud Zottegem 55
Oudenaarde Special 55
Owd Roger 83

Pabst 115
Paine 79
Pale (Staropramen) 27
Pale Ale (Moosehead) 105
Pale Ale (Samuel Smith) 81
Pale Ale (Sierra Nevada) 111
Palmer 85
Panther 98

Paracelsus 98
Paske Bryg 49
Paulaner 43-44
Pearl 124
Pedigree 83
Peeterman 60
Pelforth 93
Pelican Export 93
Pentland 87
Penrhos 84
Perlweizen (Riegele) 44
Perry's 96
Phoenix 90
Pickett 115-116
Pinkus Müller 33
Pils (Brand) 68
Pils (De Kroon) 69
Pils (De Ridder) 70
Pils Felsenkeller) 31-32
Pils (Gösser) 97
Pils (Reininghaus) 98
Pilsener (Budel) 68
Pilsener (De Leeuw) 70
Pilsener (F.X. Matt) 121
Pilskrone (Dortmunder Kronen) 35
Pilsner see also Pilsener
Pilsner (Aass) 49
Pilsner (Grolsch) 68
Pilsner Urquell 26-27
Platzl Spezial 40
Plymouth Heavy 85
Point 116
Polar Beer 51-52
Polland 79
Porter (Aass) 49
Porter (Bruce's) 76
Porter (De Bakker) 110
Porter (Labatt) 104
Porter (New Albion) 110
Porter (Samuel Smith) 87
Porter (Timothy Taylor) 81
Pottsville Porter 123
Premium (Diekirch) 65
Prinz Bräu 100
Prior Double Dark 122
Prior (St. Sixtus) 57
Pripps 52
Provisie 55
Puntigam Marzen 98

Rainier 111
Ram Tam 81
Ratskeller Eden-Pils 33
Record (33) 94
Red Dragon Dark 86
Red Label (Cascade) 128
Red Stripe 125
Red, White and Blue 115
Regal Bräu 114
Regal Christmas 63
Reininghaus 98
Reserve Saint Landelin 114
Reuze (Pelforth) 93
Ridley 79

Riegele 44
Ringnes 52
Ritter Export 35
River City 111
Robinson 79
Rochefort 65
Rocky Cellar 99
Rodenbach 55-56
Rolling Rock 121
Rothenburg 95
Royal Denmark 52
Royal Oak 85
Ruddle's of Rutland 79

Sagres 100
Saint Austell 85
St. Bernardus 57
Saint Landelin 94
St. Léonard 10, 94
St. Pauli 29-30
St. Sixtus/Bernardus
  Pater 57
Saison Dupont 63
Saison Régal 63
Saisons de Pipaix 63
Salvator (Paulaner) 44
Samichlaus 95
Samson 25
Samuel Smith 80-81
San Miguel 100, 132,
  133
Sanwald Altbier 40
Sanwald Diät Lager 40
Sanwald Weizen Krone
  40
Sapporo 132
Schell 116
Schlenkerla 44-45
Schlitz 116-117
Schmidt 121-122
Schneider 45
Schoenling 117
Schultheiss 47
Schumacher Altbier 37
Scottish & Newcastle
  71
Selecta XV (San
  Miguel) 100
70/-(Belhaven) 86-87
70/-Heavy (Maclay) 87
70/-(Lorimer) 87
Sheaf Stout 130
Shepherd Neame 76-77
Shiner Premium 124
Siegel Pils 36
Sierra Nevada 111
Simon 65
Simonds Farsons Cisk
  101
Singha 134
Siravar 26
6X 85
1664 de Kronenbourg
  93
1664 Reinheitsgebot 93
60/-(Belhaven) 86-87
60/-Light (Maclay) 87
Skol 70
Skol (Labatt) 104
Sleutel 69
Smithwick's 90
Snowflake 132

South Australian
  Brewing 129
Southwark Bitter 129
Spaten 45-46
Special Dutch 69
Special Export
  (Heileman) 114
Spezi (Riegele) 44
Spezial (Gösser) 97
Spezial (Stiegl) 98
Speziator (Riegele) 44
Spoetzl 124
Springfield Bitter 84
Stag 77
Stefanibock 97
Steffl Export 97
Steinlager 129
Stella Artois 59
Sticke Alt 37
Stiegl 98
Stifts Export 35
Stiftsbräu 97
Stingo 77
Stoney's 121
Stout (Cascade) 128
Stout (New Albion) 110
Straub 122
Stroh's 117
Strong Ale (Belhaven)
  87
Strong Brown (Samuel
  Smith) 81
Strong Golden (Samuel
  Smith) 81
Strongarm 79
Sun Lik 133
Sunderland Draught
  Bitter 82
Suntory 132
Super Dortmunder
  (Alfa) 67
Super Leeuw 69
Svetovar 26
Swan 129

Tally Ho 78
Taylor Walker 76
Ten Penny Stock Ale
  105
Tennent's Lager 88
Tetley 81
Thai Amarit 134
Theakston 81
Thier Export 35
33 94
Thomas Hardy's Ale 85
Three Town Export 52
Three Tuns 84
Thwaites 82
Tiger Beer 132, 133
Tiger Head 122
Timmermans 62
Timothy Taylor 81
Tmavé 25
Tolly 79
Toohey's Old 128
Tooth 130
Trappists of Chimay 64
Trappists of Orval 64-
  65
Trappists of Rochefort
  65

Trappists of St. Sixtus
  57
Trappists of
  Schaapskool 70
Trappists of Westmalle
  57
Traquair House 88
Tripel (Trappists of
  Westmalle) 57
Trumans 73
Tsingtao Brewery
  131-132
Tuborg 52
Tucher 46
Tusker 77
Tusker Lager 134
12-Horse 120

U Fleků 27
Ueli 95
Union beer 101
Union 63
Ur-Märzen (Spaten)
  45-46
Urtyp (Paulaner) 44

van Vollenhoven's
  Stout 69
Vanderlinden 62
Varsity 74
Vaux 82
Victoria Bitter 128
Vieille Villers Tripel 57
Vieux Temps 59
Voison 63

Wadworth 85
Walter 117
Warteck 95
Watney 77
West End Bitter 129
West Riding 81
Wethered Bitter 77
Weihenstephan 46
Weihnachts Christmas
  beer 44
Whitbread 77
Wielemans 59
Winter Royal 77
Winston 63
Winter Warmer 78
Witkap Pater Tripel 57
Worthington White
  Shield 83
Würher 100
Würzburger Hofbräu
  46-47

X-pert 69

Yates & Jackson 80
Yebisu 132
Young 77-78
Younger's IPA 87
Yuengling 123

Žatec Red 65
Zipfer Urtyp 97
Zum Schlüssel 37
Zum Uerige 37
Zywiec/Krakus 99